1993
A-che

WITHDRAWN

CITY OF CERRITOS
PUBLIC LIBRARY

1995

DEMCO
OCT 14 1998
OCT 14 1998

In the Heart of Filipino America

The Asian American Experience

Spacious Dreams
The First Wave of Asian Immigration

Journey to Gold Mountain
The Chinese in 19th-Century America

Raising Cane
The World of Plantation Hawaii

Issei and Nisei
The Settling of Japanese America

From the Land of Morning Calm
The Koreans in America

Ethnic Islands
The Emergence of Urban Chinese America

In the Heart of Filipino America
Immigrants from the Pacific Isles

India in the West
South Asians in America

Democracy and Race
Asian Americans and World War II

Strangers at the Gates Again
Asian American Immigration After 1965

From Exiles to Immigrants
The Refugees from Southeast Asia

Breaking Silences
Asian Americans Today

Lives of Famous Asian Americans
Arts/Entertainment/Sports

Lives of Famous Asian Americans
Business/Science/Politics

Lives of Famous Asian Americans
Literature and Education

E
184
.F4
T34
1994
c.2

THE ASIAN AMERICAN EXPERIENCE

In the Heart of Filipino America

IMMIGRANTS FROM THE PACIFIC ISLES

3 1230 00347 1063

Ronald Takaki

PROFESSOR OF ETHNIC STUDIES
THE UNIVERSITY OF CALIFORNIA AT BERKELEY

Adapted by Rebecca Stefoff

WITH CAROL TAKAKI

Chelsea House Publishers

New York  *Philadelphia*

On the cover A Filipino family in traditional dress, photographed in Hawaii in the 1930s.

Chelsea House Publishers

EDITORIAL DIRECTOR Richard Rennert
EXECUTIVE MANAGING EDITOR Karyn Gullen Browne
COPY CHIEF Robin James
PICTURE EDITOR Adrian G. Allen
ART DIRECTOR Robert Mitchell
MANUFACTURING DIRECTOR Gerald Levine

The Asian American Experience

SENIOR EDITOR Jake Goldberg
SERIES DESIGN Marjorie Zaum

Staff for *In the Heart of Filipino America*
EDITORIAL ASSISTANT Kelsey Goss
PICTURE RESEARCHER Sandy Jones

Adapted and reprinted from *Strangers from a Different Shore,* © 1989 by Ronald Takaki, by arrangement with the author and Little, Brown and Company, Inc.

Text © 1995 by Ronald Takaki. All rights reserved. Printed and bound in the United States of America.

First Printing
1 3 5 7 9 8 6 4 2

Library of Congress Cataloging-in-Publication Data
Takaki, Ronald T., 1939–
In the heart of Filipino America: immigrants from the Pacific isles / Ronald Takaki.
p. cm.—(The Asian American experience)
Includes bibliographical references and index.
ISBN 0-7910-2187-4.
ISBN 0-7910-2191-2 (pbk.)
1. Filipino Americans—History. 2. United States—Emigration and immigration—History—19th century. 3. United States—Emigration and immigration—History—20th century. 4. Philippines—Emigration and immigration—History—19th century. 5. Philippines—Emigration and immigration—History—20th century. [1. Filipino Americans—History.] I. Title. II. Series: Asian American experience (New York, N.Y.)
E184.F4T34 1994 94-2643
973'.049921—dc20 CIP
AC

Contents

Filipino immigrants in Seattle, around 1930.

Introduction

From a Different Shore

AS A CHILD IN HAWAII, I GREW UP IN A MULTICULTURAL corner of America. My own family had roots in Japan and China.

Grandfather Kasuke Okawa arrived in Hawaii in 1866, and my father, Toshio Takaki, came as a 13-year-old boy in 1918. My stepfather, Koon Keu Young, sailed from China to the islands when he was a teenager.

My neighbors were Japanese, Chinese, Hawaiian, Filipino, Portuguese, and Korean. Behind my house, Alice Liu and her friends played the traditional Chinese game of mahjongg late into the night, the clicking of the tiles lulling me to sleep.

Next to us the Miuras flew billowing and colorful carp kites on Japanese boy's day. I heard voices with different accents, different languages, and saw children of different colors.

Together we went barefoot to school and played games like baseball and *jan ken po*. We spoke "pidgin English," a melodious language of the streets and community. "Hey, da kind tako ono, you know," we would say, combining English, Japanese, and Hawaiian. "This octopus is delicious." Racially and culturally diverse, we all thought of ourselves as Americans.

But we did not know why families representing such an array of nationalities from different shores were living together and sharing their cultures and a common language. Our teachers and textbooks did not explain the diversity of our community or the sources of our unity.

After graduation from high school, I attended a college in a midwestern town where I found myself invited to "dinners for foreign students" sponsored by local churches and clubs like the Rotary. I politely tried to explain to my kind hosts that I was not a "foreign student." My fellow students and even my professors would ask me how long I had been in America and where I had learned to speak English. "In this country," I would reply. And sometimes I would add: "I was born in America, and my family has been here for three generations."

Asian Americans have been here for over 150 years. They are diverse, coming originally from countries such as China, Japan, Korea, the Philippines, India, Vietnam, Laos, and Cambodia. Many of them live in Chinatowns, the colorful streets filled with sidewalk vegetable stands and crowds of people carrying shopping bags; their communities are also called Little Tokyo, Koreatown, and Little Saigon. Asian Americans work in hot kitchens and bus tables in restaurants with elegant names like Jade Pagoda and Bombay Spice. In garment factories, Chinese and Korean women hunch over whirling sewing machines, their babies sleeping nearby on blankets. In the Silicon Valley of California, rows and rows of Vietnamese and Laotian women serve as the eyes and hands of production assembly lines for computer chip industries. Tough Chinese gang members strut on Grant Avenue in San Francisco and Canal Street in New York's Chinatown. In La Crosse, Wisconsin, Hmong refugees from Laos, now dependent on welfare, sit and stare at the snowdrifts outside their windows. Asian American engineers do complex research in the laboratories of the high-technology industries along

Route 128 in Massachusetts. Asian Americans seem to be everywhere on university campuses.

Today, Asian Americans belong to the fastest growing ethnic group in the United States. Kept out of the United States by immigration restriction laws in the 19th and early 20th centuries, Asians have recently been coming again to America. The 1965 immigration act reopened the gates to immigrants from Asia, allowing 20,000 immigrants from each country to enter every year. In the early 1990s, half of all immigrants entering annually are Asian.

The growth of the Asian American population has been dramatic: In 1960, there were only 877,934 Asians in the United States, representing a mere one half of 1% of the American people. Thirty years later, they numbered about seven million, or 3% of the population. They included 1,645,000 Chinese, 1,400,000 Filipinos, 845,000 Japanese, 815,000 Asian Indians, 800,000 Koreans, 614,000 Vietnamese, 150,000 Laotians, 147,000 Cambodians, and 90,000 Hmong. By the year 2000, Asian Americans will probably represent 4% of the total United States population. In California, Asian Americans already make up 10% of the state's inhabitants, compared with 7.5% for African Americans.

Yet very little is known about Asian Americans and their history. Many existing history books give Asian Americans only passing notice—or overlook them entirely. "When one hears Americans tell of the immigrants who built this nation," Congressman Norman Mineta of California observed, "one is often led to believe that all our forebearers came from Europe. When one hears stories about the pioneers going West to shape the land, the Asian immigrant is rarely mentioned."

Indeed, many history books have equated "American" with "white" or "European" in origin. In his prize-winning study, *The Uprooted,* Harvard historian Oscar Handlin presented—to use the book's subtitle—"the Epic Story of the Great Migrations that Made the American People." But Handlin's "epic story" completely left out the "uprooted" from lands across the Pacific Ocean and the "great migrations" from Asia that also helped to make "the American people." As Americans, we have origins in Europe, the Americas, Africa, and also Asia.

We need to include Asians in the history of America. How and why, we ask in this series, were the experiences of these various groups—Chinese, Japanese, Korean, Filipino, Asian Indian, and Southeast Asian—similar to and different from each other? Comparing the experiences of different nationalities can help us see what events were particular to a group and also highlight the experiences they all shared.

Why did Asian immigrants leave everything they knew and loved to come to a strange world so far away? They were "pushed" by hardships in the homelands and "pulled" by demands for their labor in Canada, Brazil, and especially the United States. But what were their own fierce dreams—from the first enterprising Chinese miners of the 1850s in search of "Gold Mountain" to the recent refugees fleeing frantically on helicopters and leaking boats from the ravages of war in Vietnam?

Besides their points of origin, we need to examine the experiences of Asian Americans in different geographical regions, especially Hawaii compared with the mainland. The time of arrival also shaped their lives and communities. About one million people entered the United States between the California gold rush of 1849 and the 1924 immigration act that cut off the flow of peoples from Asian countries. After a break of some 40 years, a second group numbering about four million came between 1965 and 1990. How do we compare the two waves of Asian immigration?

To answer our questions in these volumes, we must study Asian Americans as men and women with minds, wills, and voices. By "voices" we mean their own words and stories as told in their oral histories, conversations, speeches, and songs as well as their own writings—diaries, letters, newspapers, novels, and poems. We need to know the ordinary people.

So much of history has been the story of kings and elites, as if the "little people" were invisible and voiceless. An Asian American told an interviewer: "I am a second generation Korean American without any achievements in life and I have no education. What is it you want to hear from me? My life is not worth telling to anyone." Similarly, a Chinese immigrant said: "You know, it seems to me there's no use in me telling you all this! I was just a simple worker, a farm worker around here. My story is not going to interest anybody." But others realize they are worthy of attention. "What is it you want to know?" an old Filipino immigrant asked a researcher. "Talk about history. What's that . . . ah, the story of my life . . . and how people lived with each other in my time."

Their stories can enable us to understand Asians as actors in the making of history and as people entitled to dignity. "I hope this survey do a lot of good for Chinese people," a Chinese man told an interviewer from Stanford

University in the 1920s. "Make American people realize that Chinese people are humans. I think very few American people really know anything about Chinese." Elderly Asians want the younger generations to know about their experiences. "Our stories should be listened to by many young people," said a 91-year-old retired Japanese plantation laborer. "It's for their sake. We really had a hard time, you know."

The stories of Asian immigrations belong to our country's history. They need to be recorded in our history books, for they reflect the making of America as a nation of immigrants, as a place where men and women came to find a new beginning. At first, many Asian immigrants—probably most of them—saw themselves as sojourners, or temporary migrants. Like many European immigrants such as the Italians and Greeks, they came to America thinking they would be here only a short time. They had left their wives and children behind in their homelands. Their plan was to work here for a few years and then return home with money. But, after their arrival, many found themselves staying. They became settlers instead of remaining sojourners. Bringing their families to their adopted country, they began putting down new roots in America.

But, coming here from Asia, many of America's immigrants found they were not allowed to feel at home in the United States. Even their grandchildren and great-grandchildren still find they are not viewed and accepted as Americans. "We feel that we're a guest in someone else's house," said third generation Ron Wakabayashi, National Director of the Japanese American Citizens League, "that we can never really relax and put our feet on the table."

Behind Wakabayashi's complaint is the question: Why have Asian Americans been considered outsiders? America's immigrants from Pacific shores found they were forced to remain strangers in the new land. Their experiences here were profoundly different from the experiences of European immigrants. Asian immigrants had qualities they could not change or hide—the shape of their eyes, the color of their hair, the complexion of their skins. They were subjected not only to cultural and ethnic prejudice but also to racism. Unlike the Irish and other groups from Europe, Asian immigrants were not treated as individuals but as members of a group with distinctive physical characteristics. Regardless of their personal merits, they sadly discovered, they could not gain acceptance in the larger society.

Unlike European immigrants, Asians were victimized by laws and policies that discriminated on the basis of race. The Chinese Exclusion Act of 1882 barred the Chinese from coming to America because they were Chinese. The National Origins Act of 1924 totally prohibited Japanese immigration.

The laws determined not only who could come to America but also who could become citizens. Decades before Asian immigration began, the United States had already defined the complexion of its citizens: the Naturalization Law of 1790 had specified that naturalized citizenship was to be reserved for "whites." This law remained in effect until 1952. Unlike white ethnic immigrants from countries like Ireland, Asian immigrants were denied citizenship and also the right to vote.

But America also had an opposing tradition and vision, springing from the reality of racial and cultural "diversity." Ours has been, as Walt Whitman celebrated so lyrically, "a teeming Nation of nations" composed of a "vast, surging, hopeful army of workers," a new society where all should be welcomed, "Chinese, Irish, German,—all, all, without exceptions." In the early 20th century, a Japanese immigrant described in poetry a lesson that had been learned by farm laborers of different nationalities—Japanese, Filipino, Mexican, and Asian Indian:

People harvesting
Work together unaware
Of racial problems.

A Filipino immigrant laborer in California expressed a similar hope and understanding. America was, Macario Bulosan told his brother Carlos, "not a land of one race or one class of men" but "a new world" of respect and unconditional opportunities for all who toiled and suffered from oppression, from "the first Indian that offered peace in Manhattan to the last Filipino pea pickers." Asian immigrants came here, as one of them expressed it, searching for "a door into America" and seeking "to build a new life with untried materials." He asked: "Would it be possible for an immigrant like me to become a part of the American dream?"

This series invites students to learn how Asian Americans belong to the larger story of the rich multicultural mosaic called the United States of America.

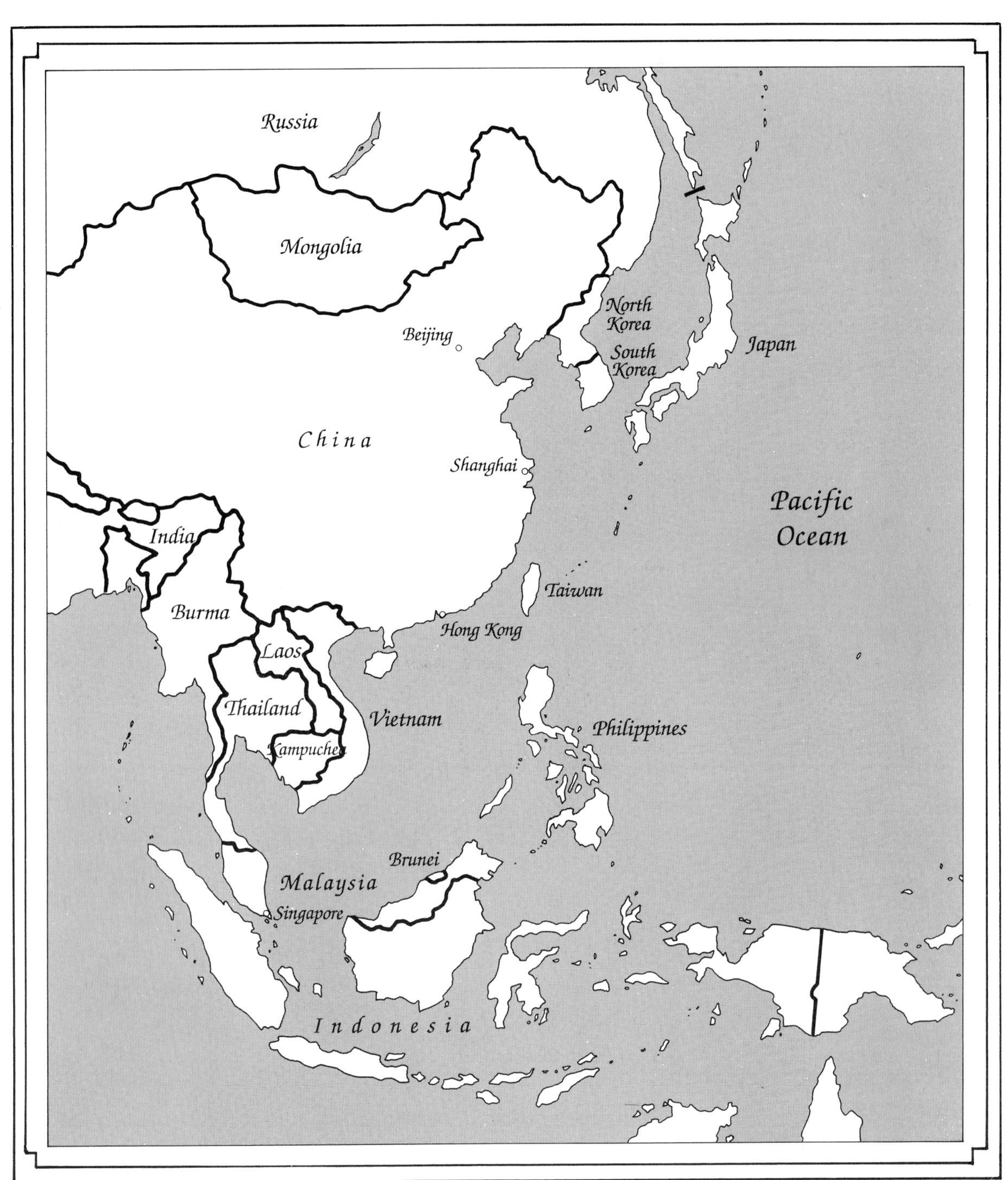

Russia
Mongolia
North Korea
Beijing
South Korea
Japan
China
Shanghai
Pacific Ocean
India
Taiwan
Burma
Hong Kong
Laos
Thailand
Vietnam
Philippines
Kampuchea
Brunei
Malaysia
Singapore
Indonesia

Thousands of Filipinos from rural villages like this one emigrated across the Pacific Ocean, pushed by poverty and pulled to America by the dream of prosperity and social equality.

Chapter One

Across the Pacific

IN THE 1920s AND 1930s, VOICES FROM THE PHILIPPINES began to be heard in the United States. The voices belonged to Filipino farm laborers in migrant work camps across the western states. In the evenings, the workers would stand outside their bunkhouses and listen to their "loneliness breathing like a tired wind over the land," as one of them said. The wind seemed to whisper a Filipino proverb: "Bravery brings many hardships." The workers had shown their courage by crossing the Pacific Ocean from their homes in the Philippine islands, but they found that life in America was full of difficulties.

As the men relaxed and stretched their sore muscles, they spoke of the loved ones they had left behind in the Philippines. During their hours of leisure, they carried bottles of wine down to the river to pick mushrooms and catch catfish for a fish fry. There, among their friends, they played guitars and sang old Filipino ballads, their voices floating across the soft night air. Some songs told of the weariness of working in the fields day after day:

Planting rice is never fun
Bent from morn till the set of sun;
Cannot stand and cannot sit
Cannot rest for a little bit.

The men also sang about coming to America and what they found there:

Then why did I have to make
A trip to this far place?
Oh! what a mistake!
At home it's easy life

For there's no task nor strife
Nor labor as hard to stand
As that in this land.

And then, filled with loneliness and memories, they sang love songs:

Will you remember
Your pledge to me
That your love
Will never be diminished?

As they sang, they felt homesick. Their voices, one Filipino later said, were "so sad, so full of yesterday and the haunting presence of familiar seas."

The Filipino immigrants came from Asia, but they came from a part of Asia that was a territory of the United States. The Philippine islands had been a Spanish colony from the 16th century to the end of the 19th century (the colony was named for King Philip II of Spain). In 1898, after defeating Spain in the Spanish-American War, the United States took control of the Philippines. The islands were to remain in American hands for nearly half a century. Filipinos were not granted U.S. citizenship, but, because they lived in a U.S. territory, they were considered "American nationals." This meant that they could emigrate to the United States and to Hawaii, which also became an American possession in 1898.

Filipinos left their homeland by the tens of thousands. In the early 1900s, they went to Hawaii to work on the sugar

In the early years, most of the Filipino emigrants were men. Girls and women remained behind in the Philippines, hoping that their sweethearts and brothers would one day return.

cane plantations. Starting in the 1920s, they also went to the U.S. mainland, where they found work in the orchards and fields of California and the fisheries of Alaska.

In some ways, the people of the Philippines were better prepared than other Asian immigrants for life in America. They had been in contact with Western culture for a long time through the Roman Catholic Church, which took root in the Philippines during the centuries of Spanish colonial rule. Many of the immigrants spoke some English in addition to Spanish and their native Filipino language.

The Filipinos were more American in their outlook than were other Asian immigrants. Many Filipinos had been educated in schools founded by Americans. "From the time of kindergarten on our islands," one man reported, "we stood in our short pants and saluted the Stars and Stripes which waved over our schoolyards." In their classrooms they looked at pictures of George Washington and Abraham Lincoln. They studied the Declaration of Independence and read English-language textbooks about the "home of the free and the land of brave."

A Filipino woman who came to the United States in 1923 recalled, "We said the 'Pledge of Allegiance' to the American flag each morning. We also sang 'The Star Spangled Banner.' All of the classes were taught in English." Thousands of American teachers had gone to the Philippine islands to Americanize the Filipinos. "I studied under American teachers, learning American history and English, being inspired by those teachers and American ideals," a Filipino told an interviewer in California in 1930. "It's no wonder that I have always wanted to come here."

Students in a history class in the Phillipines. Many of the teachers in the islands came from the United States; they taught the principles of democracy and inspired the desire to emigrate in some of their pupils.

Generally, the immigrants were laborers from poor farming families. Most of them were young men; many were teenagers. In all, far more men than women came to America in this first wave of Filipino emigration. Genevieve Laigo of Seattle never forgot how the Filipino men greatly outnumbered the women on the ship that carried them to America in 1929—there were 300 men and only 2 women! In 1930, fewer than one-fifth of the Filipinos in Hawaii were women, and only 7% of Filipinos on the U.S. mainland were women.

More Filipino women went to Hawaii than to the mainland because labor conditions were different. Filipino men were more likely to take their wives to Hawaii, where they would live and work in a permanent, stable plantation community. On the mainland, Filipino men were migratory farm laborers, moving from field to field, from one temporary camp to another, even from one state to another. This was not the sort of life most men wanted for their wives and families.

The Spanish and Catholic traditions of Filipino culture also discouraged women from leaving the Philippines in large numbers. Women travelers had to be accompanied by their husbands or fathers; it was very rare for a woman to travel on her own. In addition, many of the Filipino men who left the islands planned to be gone for only a few years before returning to the Philippines. They saw themselves as sojourners who would spend a few years in Hawaii or the United States, not as permanent settlers.

Thousands of these Filipino men had been forced by hard times to leave home. In the Philippines, said many emigrants, they found themselves "sinking down into the toilet." Life was getting harder, and people had to "reach farther and farther away to make ends meet." Times had not always been so terrible. In a poem about his early childhood in the Philippines, an immigrant in California depicted a moment of happiness and plenty:

My father was a working man
In the land of the big rains,
The water glistened on his arms
Like the cool dew in the morning
When the rice was growing tall. . . .

"In the forest behind us," a plantation laborer in Hawaii recalled as he talked about his childhood in the Philippines, "we got so much to live on. I would go hunting there with a string trap once a month and you would have to call me clumsy if I brought down less than four wild chickens. We used to trap wild pigs there too and deer." But, then, "the rich people" from town came with guns to hunt, killing all the game for sport. As time went on, peasants in the Philippines discovered that their fertile rice lands were being bought up by men who never saw their property, by "names on pieces of paper." Each year the farmers had to give a larger share of their crops to distant landlords. Many farmers were driven into debt. A Filipino immigrant remembered his father saying to his brother Luciano:

> "The moneylender has taken my land, son."
> "How much more do you owe him, Father?" asked Luciano.
> "It is one hundred pesos," said my father. "I promised to pay in three weeks, but he won't listen to me. I'd thought that by that time the rice would be harvested and I could sell some of it; then I would be able to

United States troops arrived in the Philippines in 1898 to drive the Spanish out of the islands—and stayed when the Philippines became a U.S. territory.

pay him. He sent two policemen to Mangusmana to see that I do not touch the rice. It is my own rice and land. Is it possible, son? Can a stranger take away what we have molded with our hands?"

"Yes, Father," said Luciano. "It is possible under the present government."

Many years after he had left the Philippines, another Filipino immigrant sadly described the loss of his family's land. "There was a time when my ancestors owned almost the whole town of Bulac and the surrounding villages," he said. "But when the Americans came conditions changed. Little by little my father's lands were sold. My share was mortgaged finally to keep the family from starvation and I soon found myself tilling the soil as did the poor Filipino peasants."

The farmers faced not only financial hardships but also personal abuse from the wealthier Filipinos. A young boy never forgot the day that he went with his mother into town to sell beans. There they saw an elegantly dressed young woman walking down the street. Angered by their stares, the wealthy woman rudely struck their basket with her umbrella, scattering the beans on the pavement. Crawling on her knees, the boy's mother scooped the beans into the basket. "It is all right. It is all right," she said, trying to reassure her son. Confused and stunned, the boy knew it was not all right. He knelt on the wet cement and picked the dirt and pebbles from the beans.

But there was a way out of poverty, Filipinos believed. They could go to America—Hawaii and California. "Hawaii is like a land of glory," they said. They would find work on the sugar plantations and save lots of money. Then they would return home in triumph. They would strut down the dusty streets of their villages, proudly showing off their American suits, silk shirts, and cowboy hats. They dreamed of looking rich and successful.

"Everyone," reported a Filipino immigrant, "became fascinated by the tales told of Hawaii," and were seized by what was commonly known as the "Hawaiian fever." Labor agents, called "drummers," were sent by the Hawaiian sugar

Filipino American families in Louisiana in 1909. Long before the Philippines came into U.S. hands in 1898, Filipinos had entered America by way of Spain's New World colonies. Some of them established communities in Louisiana, where they were known as Manilamen.

planters to the Philippines to spread this fever. They traveled from town to town, showing movies of the "glorious adventure and the beautiful opportunities" awaiting Filipino workers in Hawaii. These movies were free and were usually shown in the town square so that everybody could see them. A typical scene from one such movie showed workers receiving paychecks.

The labor agents "dazzled the Filipino eyes" with the sum of $2 a day, a very good wage compared with the 15 cents a man could earn for a day of hard labor in the Philippines. "The migrating Filipino," reported a newspaper in Manila, the capital of the Philippines, "sees no opportunity for him in the Philippines." Lured to the United States in the 1920s, one immigrant told an interviewer many years later, "Back home, we thought California was the Eldorado"—the legendary land of gold.

Trying to climb out of debt and servitude, Filipinos signed labor contracts. They agreed to work for three years in exchange for transportation to Hawaii and wages of $18 a month, plus housing, water, fuel, and medical care. Decades later, a Filipino man vividly remembered the day that he signed his labor contract:

The agent was just coming down the steps when I halted my horse in front of the recruiter's office. He was a fellow Filipino, but a Hawaiian.

"Where are you going?" he asked.

"I would like to present myself for Hawaii, Apo," I answered as I came down from my horse.

"Wait, I'll go see if I can place you on the next load," he said, and turned back up into the door.

When he came out, he had a paper in his hand. "Come up, so we can fill in the forms," he waved; so I went in.

"You write?" he asked.

"No," I said; so he filled in for me.

"Come back Monday for the doctor to check you up," he said, patting me on the back. "When you come back, bring *beinte cinco,* twenty-five, and I'll make sure of your papers for a place," he said, shaking my hand.

It was like that. "Tip" is what we call it here. But that is our custom to *pasoksok,* slipsome, for a favor.

A carpentry shop at the Philippines School of Arts and Trades in Manila. Workers in the islands, who were paid low wages, listened eagerly to tales of the fortunes to be made in Hawaii.

Those who left home promised to be gone for only three years. They believed it would be easy to save money in America. Returning with rolls of cash in their pockets, they would pay off the mortgages on their lands and recover their family homes. "My sole ambition was to save enough money to pay back the mortage on my land," explained one man. "In the Philippines a man is considered independent and is looked upon with respect by his neighbors if he possesses land." As he said farewell to his brother in the Philippines, another laborer promised, "I will come back and buy that house. I will buy it and build a high cement wall around it. I will come back with lots of money and put on a new roof. . . . Wait and see!"

But some of the departing Filipinos knew that they would not be coming back. Rufina Clemente Jenkins had met an American soldier in the Philippines during the Spanish-American War and married him in 1900. Two years later, she sailed to the United States with her daughter to join her husband and make her home with him. Angeles Amoroso also knew that she had limited opportunities for an education and jobs in the Philippines, so she decided to search for a new future in the United States. "My father had the impression I would be away only for seven years," she said later, "but I knew in my heart that I would be making America my permanent home."

By 1930, some 150,000 Filipinos had made their way to America. The majority of them went to Hawaii. They were met on the Honolulu docks by labor contractors and plantation managers, who took them to the sugar cane plantations and gave them living quarters in the plantation camps. The camps were bleak and unwelcoming, especially in the early years. The Filipinos found themselves living in shabby,

Filipino cane workers on a Hawaiian plantation. For many, the hoped-for "land of glory" turned out to be a land of struggle and exhaustion.

crowded barracks or dormitories—nothing at all like the familiar, friendly villages they had left behind.

Work, too, was different in Hawaii. Farmers in the Philippines set their own pace and decided what to do and when to do it. On the plantations, however, workers' lives were ruled by shrill steam whistles and demanding foremen. Roused before dawn, the Filipinos labored all day in the hot, dusty cane fields. "For the first two and a half years here," one Filipino laborer said, "I lived pretty much the same. Six days a week I worked from siren to siren." The moments of relaxation were cherished. A Filipino man recalled that he "went with friends to the rocky edge of the ocean" to "throw net" for fish on Sundays. Holidays and festivals brought a welcome departure from the daily routine. The most important celebration of the year was Rizal Day, December 30, a holiday that honored José Rizal, a Filipino revolutionary leader who was executed by the Spanish in 1896. Through such shared festivals and other cultural traditions, the Filipinos in Hawaii clung to a sense of ethnic identity and community.

The Filipinos were part of a multicultural society that developed on the plantations as the owners imported workers from many nations: China, Japan, Korea, and Portugal, as well as the Philippines. The plantation owners' strategy was to pit one group against the others, hoping that ethnic pride and rivalry would make the workers more productive. The owners also believed that workers of different ethnic backgrounds would not join together to form labor unions and ask for higher wages or better living conditions. As part of this strategy, Filipino laborers were sometimes used to break strikes by Japanese workers. When Japanese workers formed a union and demanded higher wages, the planters replaced many of them with Filipino workers.

Yet the Filipino workers, too, formed their own labor union. At first each union operated on its own. In 1920, however, the labor movement in Hawaii took a big step forward when Pablo Manlapit, the Filipino union leader, called for Filipino and Japanese workers to unite. "We should work on this strike shoulder to shoulder," he declared. His call was answered. More than 8,000 Filipino and Japanese workers joined together in Hawaii's first interethnic strike. By rising above ethnic boundaries, these workers were helping to create the diverse but unified society of modern multicultural Hawaii.

Hawaii was not the only destination for the Filipino immigrants. Nearly one-third of them sailed farther east, to the U.S. mainland. There they found themselves in a new and challenging world of work, of prejudice, and of opportunity. This is their story.

More than half of all Filipino immigrants in the mainland United States in the 1930s were farm laborers. They traveled throughout the West, planting and picking all kinds of crops.

Chapter Two

The World of Work

THE FILIPINOS APPEARED SUDDENLY AND SWIFTLY ON the American mainland. In 1910, there were only 400 of them on the mainland. Many had come recently as students, but some were the Louisiana descendents of Spanish-speaking Filipinos who had deserted Spanish ships in the 18th century. Ten years later, in 1920, there were 5,600 Filipinos on the mainland, and, ten years after that, there were 40,000. Filipinos were almost everywhere: in Washington, Oregon, Michigan, Illinois, New York, Colorado, Kansas, Virginia, Maryland, Pennsylvania, Mississippi, Montana, Idaho, Texas, and Arizona. The majority of them, however, settled in California, which was the main point of entry for immigrants from across the Pacific. The Filipino population of California jumped from 5 in 1910 to 30,500 in 1930.

Arriving in San Francisco, the newcomers saw taxis waiting for them near the docks, ready to drive them to Stockton, in the Central Valley, the heart of California's agricultural region. They could have taken the bus or train to Stockton for $2, but most of them found themselves swept into taxis, four or five Filipinos in each taxi, together paying $65 to $75 for the trip to Stockton—the gathering place for Filipinos as they came to America. "We landed in San Francisco," an immigrant recalled. "An uncle met us and took us to Stockton because that was the center of labor for our kind of people, that worked in the field."

When Manuel Buaken arrived in Stockton, he found the city "flooded with Filipinos." In his book *I Have Lived with the American People,* he described how these immigrants had "come in search of that big money they had heard about, believing the same fantastic tales. . . . They were all waiting for calls to work on the farms, and in the meantime, they had no money and could only bum their way in and around the city." From Stockton, the Filipinos fanned out into three kinds of jobs—domestic service, the fisheries of the Pacific Northwest and Alaska, and agriculture.

One-fourth of the Filipinos on the mainland in 1930 were service workers. They were janitors, valets, kitchen helpers, pantrymen, dishwashers, bellboys, houseboys, elevator boys, door boys, and busboys. "My husband worked in a restaurant as a busboy," said one woman. "That's the only kind of job he was allowed to have." According to Buaken, who worked as a dishwasher in Pasadena's Huntington Hotel, white people took unskilled jobs as dishwashers and porters "only as a last resort, but the Filipino knew he must take these for keeps, because this was the only type of work open to him in the United States." As servants, Filipinos were expected to behave in an especially lowly manner. "I had to crawl on my knees to please them [white employers]," a Filipino busboy confided. "I had to be submissive and servile and eternally patient; had to be known for my whole-hearted willingness to serve others—or else! The laborer is not worthy of his hire, unless he also smiles."

Nearly one-tenth of the Filipinos worked in the Alaska salmon fisheries. Recruited on the West Coast by Japanese and Filipino labor contractors, they were hired for the "long season" of seven months beginning in April, or for the "extra season" of three months from June through August. In 1930, 15% of all workers in Alaska's fisheries were Filipinos. These Alaskeros, as they were called, cleaned salmon and packed them in boxes, working six days a week, from six o'clock in the morning until six o'clock at night. Their few leisure hours were lonely times. The "Song of the Alaskero" describes their life and labor in the salmon industry:

It's a hard lonesome fate
We face in Alaska.
Oh! what a fate!
Stale fat and ill-cooked fish,
Our major, daily dish . . .
From the stingy, bossy Chink
Give us tummy-ache.

We may curl and be bold
Beneath some cover thick.
Yet oh! how cold!

A Filipino tailoring shop in Stockton, California, a city that served as a major gathering place for immigrants from the islands.

And then ere the break of day
Though dog tired we may be
Up we must willy-nilly
For another day.

After the fishing season was over, the Alaskeros returned to Seattle or San Francisco. Usually, they were disappointed to find that they had not actually made much money, because their employers subtracted large amounts from their wages to pay for their food and other expenses in Alaska. Most Filipinos had borrowed money from labor contractors so they could go to Alaska and work. But when they came back to the

"Oh! What a fate!" lamented the Alaskeros, the Filipinos who toiled in the salmon canneries of Alaska. Theirs was dirty, dangerous work with little profit.

West Coast, they were broke. They had to borrow from the contractors just to eat, so they were forced to sign up for another season in Alaska. As one Alaskero said, they did "the same thing, year in and year out, season after season."

More than half of all Filipinos in the United States worked in agriculture. They were organized into work gangs or crews led by Filipino labor contractors, who found the jobs and set the men's wages with the growers. "You would have one crew boss who would be in charge of all the 'boys,'" explained an immigrant. "In the old days, he would go around to the different farmers and say, 'Do you need some work done? I can bring in my crew. My company comes out to over forty, fifty people.'" Riding in old cars and trucks, they moved from field to field to harvest the ripening fruit and vegetables.

"We traveled. I mean we moved from camp to camp," a Filipino said. He explained that the work year began in January, with asparagus picking. After the asparagus season, the laborers worked in orchards, picking fruit. Most of the workers were men, but there were a few women, and even children, who stood on boxes to pick fruit for hours at a time. In California, they moved from Salinas to Manteca, Stockton, Lodi, Fresno, Delano, Dinuba, San Luis Obispo, Imperial, and Sacramento, cutting spinach here, picking strawberries there. They went on to Montana, where they harvested beets. In Idaho, they dug potatoes. In Washington's Yakima Valley, they picked apples, and in Oregon, they hoed hops, a plant used for making beer.

Fieldwork in the American West was harder than anything they had known in the Philippines. "I worked about six hours that first day," a Filipino laborer recalled, "and when my back was hurting I said to myself: 'Why did I come to this

Filipino farm laborers discovered a new spirit of unity and purpose when they formed a union to demand better wages and working conditions.

country? I was doing easy in the Philippines.'" He kept hoping that he would get used to the work. "But boy, the next day I could hardly sit down because my back and all of my body was sore."

The workday was long. Laborers moved into the fields at daybreak and returned to their camps after sundown. The temperature in the fields seemed hotter than it had ever been in the Philippines. A Filipino described working in California's vineyards: "It was one hundred and thirteen degrees. I used to get two gallons of water to pour on my head. By the time it reached the ground, I was dry."

As they worked, Filipinos were sometimes choked by clouds of dust. "How dusty it was and itchy," one immigrant recalled. "Peat dirt even went inside your shoes, no matter how tight your shoes. If you wore hightops, when you took your shoes off, you saw about [an] inch of dust inside." The blowing dust settled in the workers' ears, noses, and eyes. Said one, "I know from personal experience that when the sun beats down on the backs of the workers, the perspiration combined with the dust becomes almost unbearably itchy."

Filipinos harvested a wide variety of crops, including cotton, oranges, tomatoes, celery, onions, peas, melons, and lettuce. Above all, however, they picked asparagus. A woman who worked in the asparagus fields remembered how the Filipinos' day began at four o'clock in the morning. The workers went out into the fields "with flashlights on their heads just like miners." The gangs of cutters numbered as many as 300 workers. On hot, dry days, they were surrounded by the fine soil that was ideal for asparagus growing, but on rainy, wet days, they carried heavy loads of mud on their boots as they trudged along the rows, stooping to gather the delicate shoots.

Planting cauliflower was also tiresome, backbreaking work. Laborers followed a wagon that stopped every so often to drop handfuls of cauliflower seedlings between the long furrows. Bent over, workers picked up the seedlings with one hand and dug into the ground with the other. Then they moved on to dig the next hole.

Filipinos were viewed by farmers as ideally suited for "stoop labor," such as cutting asparagus and planting cauliflower. In 1930, the editor of a California newspaper said, "White men can't do the work as well as these short men who can get down on their hands and knees, or work all day long stooping over." A farmer said that he used Filipinos for stoop labor because they were "small and work fast." But a Filipino laborer disputed these racist notions, saying, "Many people think that we don't suffer from stoop labor, but we do."

At six o'clock in the evening, the workers climbed into wagons and were taken away from the fields. Always they returned to their camps covered with dirt. Their bodies were

Filipino workers on a California asparagus farm.

sweaty and itchy; they could hardly wait for their bath. But sometimes the wait was a long one. One Filipino recalled the bathing arrangement in a work camp:

> [There was] only one bath tub to be filled with water heated in large individual galvanized cans for the one hundred boys to use. All took a bath each day after working, for it was impossible to sleep and rest well without bathing. But, on account of the tremendous amount of work required in emptying the tub and the difficult and annoying method of heating the water for the bath, some five to ten people took a bath in the same water before it was changed. So the job of bathing one hundred boys was an ordeal. It took six hours to heat enough water to wash one hundred dirty men.

After dinner, the tired men went to bed, but many of them slept restlessly. "It was hard work," said a worker, "and at night, I'd feel all kinds of pain in my body—my back, my arm." The camps consisted of run-down bunkhouses and shacks that looked like "chicken houses." A Filipino remembered, "The bunkhouse was made of old pieces of wood and was crowded with men. There was no sewage disposal. When I ate swarms of flies fought over my plate. . . . I slept on a dirty cot: the blanket was never washed." One grower explained that he liked to hire Filipinos because they were single men and could be housed inexpensively. He said, "These Mexicans and Spaniards bring their families with them and I have to fix up houses; but I can put a hundred Filipinos in that barn," and he pointed to a large firetrap.

Sometimes Filipinos were housed in a cluster of tents. "We lived in tents with board flooring which was very convenient because when it rained, there was no mud," a worker said. "We slept in cot beds. They gave us enough blankets. It got cold at nights." It had never been that cold back home in the Philippines. Another man remembered his shock at the low temperatures of American nights: "Having just arrived from the Philippines it was hard to get used to the cooler climate. Oh man, sometimes I had to cover myself with the old mattress to stay warm through the night. It was cold, awful cold, and you could feel the wind blowing through the cracks in the wall."

Other Filipino farm laborers were not even provided with tents. They had to be resourceful. Recalled one, "You made your own house, cooked your own food, you had to make your own stove out of anything . . . the farmer didn't supply you with shelter or anything."

Filipino farm laborers did not accept these terrible working conditions. One grower complained that the Filipinos he had hired in 1924 proved to be "most unsatisfactory." They were, he said, "the essence of independence" and demanded higher wages. An agricultural official in California reported in 1930 that after Filipinos had been in the United States for a time they became "educated and sophisticated." This made them "increasingly hard to manage."

The laborers became even harder to manage during the 1930s, when the United States entered the Great Depression, a period of widespread economic hardship. Wages fell, and the Filipinos felt trapped in "a pit of economic slavery," as Manuel Buaken put it. He asked, "What are we to do to elevate ourselves?" The answer came from the fields. When

growers in California's Imperial Valley tried to reduce wages in 1930, Filipino and Mexican field-workers went on strike. But the growers used the government to smash the strike. Police authorities arrested more than 100 workers.

Unlike Japanese and Chinese immigrants, the Filipinos did not form large ethnic communities of their own. Their business enterprises were generally located in or near Chinatowns, like this Filipino café in Seattle's Chinatown.

Despite this setback, the labor movement continued to gather strength as farm workers resisted wage cuts. Filipinos in Stockton and Salinas formed the Filipino Labor Union (FLU). Four thousand Filipinos joined the FLU to fight low wages and racial discrimination. "Strength is in union," they said. In 1933, the FLU led a one-day strike to protest the 20-cents-an-hour wage. The growers easily broke the strike by bringing in other laborers, and relations between the FLU and the growers remained tense.

The showdown between the FLU and the growers came in 1934, when the FLU demanded that the growers recognize the workers' right to strike for higher wages. The FLU led Filipino lettuce workers in a strike, demanding 40

Field work was called "stoop labor." Working from daybreak to sundown, choking with dust, many laborers suffered from backaches and other ailments.

to 45 cents an hour, recognition for the union, and better working conditions. A total of 6,000 workers went on strike, for the Filipino strikers were joined by white workers. But interracial unity quickly broke down when the white strikers agreed to deal separately with the growers.

Facing the growers alone, the Filipino strikers felt the full force of the opposition. The growers used other Filipino laborers as scabs to replace the strikers. They also brought in Mexican laborers to break the strike and spread stories that the FLU leaders were communists. At the same time, the growers enlisted the help of highway patrolmen, local special deputies, and armed vigilantes to drive off 500 strikers. A sign in Salinas warned the striking Filipinos: "This Is a White

Man's Country. Get Out of Here if You Don't Like What We Pay."

The growers' war against the strikers reached its peak when vigilantes attacked the camp of Rufo Canete, the president of the FLU. "Get going and don't come back," they shouted as they burned the camp to the ground and forced the strikers to flee for their lives. The police then raided the union headquarters in Salinas, arresting scores of strikers and their leader. Shortly after the raid, the captain of the state highway patrol announced, "Everything is quiet, I think the strike is over. Have leader in jail."

But still the Filipino strikers held out. Finally, in order to end the strike, the growers were forced to meet some of the FLU's demands: wages of 40 cents an hour and recognition of the FLU as a legitimate farm workers' union. In 1936, the FLU organized another strike in the Salinas Valley of California. As a result of this strike, a joint Mexican-Filipino union was formed. Through the FLU, Filipinos had become an important part of the American labor movement.

Their involvement in the labor movement brought a new sense of ethnic unity to Filipinos in the United States. "There was a need for us Filipinos to organize an independent union," recalled a Filipino worker named Antonio Gallego Rodrigo, "and force the growers to give us higher wages, better working and living conditions. . . . To me, it did not matter what island [in the Philippines] they came from or what dialect they spoke. They were all Filipinos like me." As this worker and thousands of his fellow Filipinos struggled for economic justice, they grew more determined to find what they called "a door into America."

Like other Asian immigrants before them, Filipinos encountered the ugly reality of racism. They sought a "door into America," but the door was not open to people of color.

Chapter Three

Confronting Prejudice

THE FILIPINOS SOUGHT A DOOR INTO AMERICA, BUT that door was not open to them. A Filipino riddle warned newcomers: "There is a beautiful lady surrounded with swords." Immigrants from the Philippines had expected to find America beautiful and generous, but instead they found the country ringed by sharp blades of hostility and prejudice. "I have been four years in America," a Filipino immigrant in California said sadly, "and I am still a stranger. It is not because I want to be. I have tried to be as 'American' as possible. I live like an American, eat like American, and dress the same, and yet everywhere I find Americans who remind me of the fact that I am a stranger." He and his fellow Filipinos had come to the United States thinking they were Americans, only to find that many whites treated them with contempt.

To most white people of the time, the Filipinos seemed to be inferior. Explaining why he had decided that the United States should take over the Philippines, President William McKinley said that it was America's duty to "educate" and "uplift" the Filipinos. The people of the Philippines were seen as backward natives to be "civilized," as "little brown brothers" who needed the guidance of the more "advanced" white Americans. But within the United States, the notion of white racial supremacy led some Americans to view the Filipinos far less kindly. "It must be realized that the Filipino is just the same as the manure that we put on the land—just the same," the secretary of an agricultural association said in 1930. "He is not our 'little brown brother.' He is no brother at all!—he is not our social equal."

Like other Asian immigrants, Filipinos experienced racial discrimination in the United States. Often they found themselves mistaken for the Asian groups that had entered the country earlier. "Because of my color and race the white man mistakes me for either a Japanese or Chinese," a Filipino said. When a Filipino tried to get a haircut, he was asked by the white barber if he was Japanese. After he had been refused service in a white-owned barbershop, an immigrant named Magdaleno Abaya was hurt and frightened. He said, "Whenever I wanted to go into an American barber shop I always hesitated for fear that I would be treated like a dog again."

On the doors of hotels, Filipinos often read signs saying, "Positively No Filipinos Allowed." Sometimes they were kept from entering theaters or forced to sit in segregated sections. For example, the Broadway Theater in Portland segregated Asians and black people in the balcony section, allowing "only whites on the first floor." Filipinos were often refused service in restaurants. Entering a coffee shop in San Francisco, Roberto Vallangca sat down and waited to be served. "The two waitresses simply ignored me, laughing and joking with the other customers—acting like I was not there," he bitterly recalled. "Other customers came and went—some even sat beside me. The waitresses served them but did not even bother to even talk to or look at me. After about twenty-five minutes, I left the shop, feeling low, sad, ashamed; I realized then that I could not go anywhere because I was a Filipino."

Finding a place to live was usually a frustrating ordeal. Landlords and realtors said things, such as "Orientals are not allowed here" and "Only whites are allowed in this neighborhood." One Filipino was told, "The reason why Orientals are not allowed to rent a place here is the fear that the place might be overcrowded with other nationalities. You were not the first one to try to rent a place here. I have other Filipinos, as well as Japanese, Chinese, and Mexicans in my office, and always I have to turn them away."

Filipinos could not buy land, either. Land laws in California and other states said that only people who were

One of the many Filipino bands that traveled among the campos, or work camps, providing entertainment for parties and festivals.

eligible to become U.S. citizens could own land—and a federal law dating from 1790 declared that only "white" immigrants could become citizens. Like the Japanese, Chinese, Koreans, and Asian Indians, Filipinos were not "white." They could not become citizens, and therefore they could not buy property in their own names. They could, however, purchase property in the names of their children born in the United States, who were automatically U.S. citizens. "My folks were not citizens," said Terry Rosal, "so they could not buy a house. They bought the house, but the house was under my name and my brother, George, and still is. . . . They could never own a farm. They were just laborers, working in the agricultural fields."

Antonio and Angeles Mendoza, who wanted to buy a house in Oakland, California, received special help from their landladies. They had been renting an apartment from two Irish sisters. The sisters worried about the young Filipino couple, knowing that as Asians they would not be able to buy a home. So the landladies secretly saved the rent money each month and used it to buy a house for the young people as a gift. "That's how we got to own a house," Angeles Mendoza explained. "One of the white families tried to circulate a petition demanding we move out of the neighborhood, but no other families would sign it."

Over and over again, Filipinos encountered negative stereotypes and images. Even though the arrest rate for Filipino men was lower than that for white men, Filipinos were often seen as "criminally-minded," as troublemakers, willing to "slash, cut or stab at the least provocation." They were called "headhunters" and "untamed," primitive savages. The

Founding members of the Filipino Cannery Workers' and Farm Laborers' Union, part of the American Federation of Labor, in 1933. Filipinos made a significant contribution to the American labor movement.

head of a government commission on immigration shared these prejudices. He called the Filipino immigrants "jungle folk" with a "primitive moral code."

Filipinos protested against this sort of racial prejudice. They pointed out that it was in conflict with America's ideals. One Filipino spokesperson declared, "We do not find that the United States government puts its theories into practice. In school in the Islands we learn from the Declaration of Independence that all men are created equal. But when we get over here we find people treating us as if we were inferior."

White prejudice was fueled by competition between whites and Filipinos for jobs. This ethnic labor rivalry often erupted into racial violence and riots. A Filipino said, "We were driving them [white workers] out of their jobs and they hated us. They'd gang up on us in the streets, shouting 'monkey, monkey.'" In Washington's Yakima Valley in 1928, 150 white workers stopped 60 Filipinos on their way to pick apples. The angry mob escorted the Filipinos out of the area and told them to keep going or be shot. Elsewhere in Washington State, Filipinos were assaulted and beaten by white mobs.

Anti-Filipino hate and violence were most intense in California. Noting the attacks on Filipino laborers in 1929, a newspaper in the Salinas Valley predicted that conflict between whites and Filipinos would soon "break forth in a nasty eruption." White workers' resentment against Filipino laborers grew worse during the Great Depression of the 1930s as the economy collapsed and jobs became scarce. Afraid and angry, white workers threatened to take the law into their own hands. The chief of police in one California town received a letter warning, "Get rid of all Filipinos or we'll burn this town down." A farmer received a similar threatening message. It said, "Work no Filipinos or we'll destroy your crop and you too."

In Reedley, California, 100 Filipino laborers were asleep in their camp in December when a dynamite bomb was thrown at them by white men in a passing car. After the attack, the owner of the farm said, "I told the boys in the camp to defend themselves if they had to." Another farmer said that his Filipino men would not go to work without their guns. A few months after the bomb-throwing incident, another bomb was thrown into a barn in Imperial, California, where 75 Filipino workers were housed. The explosion killed a laborer and wounded several others. One Filipino never forgot the moment of horror. "When we arrived home, we were bombarded with stones thrown by a white mob," he said. "They threw a stone into our kitchen. They didn't like Filipinos to stay in that town. [The next day] about nine o'clock, we went to bed. My gosh, about fifteen minutes [later], I heard a bomb . . . under the garage. Aresto Lande was killed. He was hit by the dynamite. His stomach was just a hole."

Complaining about Filipino labor competition, a white worker told an interviewer in 1930, "Why, I applied just the other day for a job at a fruit ranch, and the superintendent told me: 'The hours are long, the pay is small, and you're not the right color anyway.' Can you beat that? . . . He said, 'I have orders to employ men—lots of 'em, but they have to be Mexicans and Filipinos.'" The frustrated white laborer continued, "It's no telling what these Filipinos will do if they keep comin'; and it's no tellin' what the 'white' man will do either. Something is liable to happen."

Something had already happened at Watsonville, California, where a bloody anti-Filipino race riot exploded in December 1929. The police saw a Filipino man with a white teenage girl and arrested him. He was released from jail after the girl's mother explained that her daughter and the Filipino man were engaged with her approval. The town newspaper published a picture of the couple embracing each other, and a month later, local businesspeople protested against the presence of Filipino immigrants. They called Filipinos "a moral and sanitary" threat and "a menace to white labor." A local judge described Filipinos in crude, racist terms. Fifteen of them, he said, would live in "one room and content themselves with squatting on the floor eating rice and fish,"

Alaskeros on strike in Seattle in 1939. Workers had succeeded in getting rid of the labor contractors who took a portion of their wages; cannery bosses now had to deal with the unions.

but he neglected to point out that Filipinos lived in crowded rooms because this was all that their employers provided. The judge also warned that Filipino men were dangerously attractive to white girls.

Remarks like these by white leaders in Watsonville whipped up a frenzy of anti-Filipino feeling that erupted into violence. Four hundred white men attacked a Filipino dance hall. During four terrible days of rioting, many Filipinos were beaten and one was shot to death.

Shortly after the riot, the same judge blamed the Filipinos for provoking the violence. "Damn the Filipino! He won't keep his place," the judge exclaimed in an interview. In an article on the riot, a writer for a Baltimore newspaper said, "The Filipinos got into trouble at Watsonville because they . . . danced better, and spent their money more lavishly than their Nordic fellow farmhands and, therefore, appealed more than some of the latter to the local girls."

The fury against Filipinos stemmed not just from rivalry over jobs but also from fears about sexual relations between Filipino men and white women. Unlike men from China, Japan, Korea, and India, men from the Philippines seemed to seek out white female companionship and to be attractive to white women. "The Filipinos are . . . a social menace as they will not leave our white girls alone and frequently intermarry," a white man testified to a congressional committee on immigration in 1930. He added that he had recently been at an automobile show in Washington, D.C., where he had seen something he had never expected to see: "As we were looking at some of the nicer cars along comes a Filipino and a nice looking white girl. We followed them around to be sure we were not mistaken. . . . I don't know what she saw in him."

To this man and others who shared his views, relationships between Filipino men and white women threatened white racial purity. Many white Americans were enraged at the sight of Filipino men in the company of white women. Filipino men who dated white women had to worry about harassment and physical abuse from white men. "Once we went out with white people, white children, or especially the girls, we were in a dangerous spot," said one man. "The life of the young Filipino at that time was very sad. We were not even allowed to go to the public dances without being bothered." Another man explained, "If you dated a white woman, you didn't know what was going to happen. You were scared in public." Filipino men were especially afraid of the police. One man said, "The law said we could not go out with white women. So you got to sneak. You hide, you sneak because the police will see you. They might put you in jail."

Since 1880, California had had a law against marriages between whites and "Negroes, mulattoes, or Mongolians." A newspaper in Stockton claimed that Filipinos were Mongolians and were "obviously" prohibited from intermarrying with whites. The writer went on to say that although the "little brown brothers" might flock to American shores, they could never blend into American society, and intermarriage with whites "would be unthinkable." California's attorney general warned that the law against racial intermarriage should apply to Filipinos so that the purity of the white race would be preserved. The state legislature revised its law against racial intermarriage to ban marriages between whites and Filipinos. Twelve other states also outlawed such marriages. Couples who wished to marry had to travel to states where intermarriage was legal.

Another form of discrimination involved citizenship. Filipinos were denied the right to become U.S. citizens because a 1790 federal law said that only "white" immigrants were allowed to become naturalized citizens. In 1934, the United States Supreme Court upheld that law, declaring that only immigrants who belonged to "the Caucasian race" could become naturalized U.S. citizens. According to the Supreme Court, "the Chinese, the Japanese, the Hindus, the American Indians and the Filipinos" were excluded from citizenship.

Julian Ilar, a Filipino student at the University of Chicago, bitterly observed:

> Try as we will we cannot become Americans. We may go to the farthest extreme in our effort to identify ourselves with the ways of the Americans . . . but nevertheless we are not able to shake off that tenacious psychology. Always we remain sensitive, always we retain at least a subconscious fear that we are being slighted because we are Filipinos. Always there lurks over us a trace of suspicion that perhaps after all, we do not "belong."

Exclusionists—white Americans who wanted to keep other races out of the country—indeed felt that Filipinos did not "belong." The exclusionists believed that Filipinos should not be permitted to immigrate to the United States. But the exclusionists faced a legal problem. In 1924, Congress had passed a federal law that banned all Asian immigration. This law could not be applied to Filipinos, however, because they came from an American territory.

Filipinos presented California with a serious "race problem," explained a white professor in 1931. Other Asian races had been excluded by the 1924 immigration law, but the Filipino "problem" was different. Filipinos could not become citizens, but neither could they be kept from entering the country, for they were governed by the United States. The only way to exclude Filipinos, the professor said, was to grant independence to the Philippines.

Three years later, in 1934, the Congress passed the Tydings-McDuffie Act. The act changed the status of the Philippines from a territory to a commonwealth—in other words, it gave the Philippines a greater degree of independence, although the islands were still under overall American control. The act also declared that the Philippines would receive complete independence in 10 years. "The Pacific coast states have resolved to bring about Filipino exclusion," a Filipino newspaper in Los Angeles commented. "Since they could not achieve that result except by giving the Philippines independence, they must now vote . . . for independence."

Ironically, at a time when many colonies and territories around the world had to resort to revolution or protest to win independence from Western powers, the United States was eager to grant independence to the Philippines. As residents of an independent country rather than a U.S. territory, Filipinos would no longer be able to enter the United States freely. Senator Millard Tydings, one of the authors of the Tydings-McDuffie Act, argued for Filipino exclusion, saying, "It is absolutely illogical to have an immigration policy to exclude Japanese and Chinese and permit Filipinos en masse to come into the country. . . . If they continue to settle in certain areas they will come in conflict with white labor . . .

and increase the opportunity for more racial prejudice and bad feeling of all kinds."

Under the new law, Filipino immigration was limited to only 50 people each year. Additional Filipinos would be allowed to enter Hawaii as plantation laborers whenever the sugar planters required them, but Filipinos in Hawaii were prohibited from coming to the U.S. mainland. Furthermore,

White women found Filipino men attractive—a fact that added fuel to the fire of racial discrimination. Many whites were angered by the sight of Asian and white people together at dances or on dates.

the Tydings-McDuffie Act said that Filipinos in the United States were "aliens," or citizens of another country, instead of U.S. nationals.

As soon as they were reclassified as aliens, Filipinos suddenly found themselves cut off from the welfare programs that many Americans depended on during the bleak years of the Great Depression. A welfare law of 1937 declared that aid went first to American citizens in need of help and next to needy aliens who planned to become citizens. But Filipinos had been told by the Supreme Court that they could not even apply for citizenship because they were not "white." As a result, thousands of hungry and poor Filipinos were unable to receive federal aid.

In truth, laws designed to keep Filipinos out of the United States were not really needed by the time the Tydings-McDuffie Act was passed in 1934. Filipinos were no longer coming to the country in significant numbers. America's image as the promised land had faded for Filipinos. In 1930, the Bureau of Labor in the Philippines reported, "Widespread publicity has been given to the newspaper accounts of labor disturbances [in America] and to the fact that there is a great deal of unemployment and suffering among the Filipinos in the western part of the United States. The true facts regarding the situation are now becoming generally known and there is much less tendency for adventurous young Filipinos to go the United States." The number of Filipino immigrants to the United States dropped suddenly and sharply from 11,400 in 1929 to only 1,300 in 1932.

Still, the exclusionists were not satisfied. They wanted the 45,000 Filipinos who were already in America to be removed. In Los Angeles, for example, a city official called for

7,000 poor Filipinos to be deported, or sent out of the country. In 1935, Congress responded to the demands of the exclusionists by passing the Repatriation Act, a law that offered free transportation back to the Philippines to any who wished to return. In exchange for their passage to the Philippines, the Filipinos who accepted the offer would have to give up their right to come back to the United States.

The *Los Angeles Times* urged Filipinos to take advantage of the Repatriation Act and "go back home." Here, the paper said, was an opportunity to sail on "luxuriant ocean liners with Uncle Sam paying their passage and all expenses and wishing them bon voyage," and to be "greeted in Manila by brass bands and songs of welcome."

White laborers on the Pacific Coast cheered the Repatriation Act. They saw the program as "a good excuse for inviting Filipino workers to go home rather than stay in the United States, selling their services for ten cents an hour, in competition with white men." But the Repatriation Act did not live up to the exclusionists' hopes. Only 2,190 Filipinos accepted the offer.

Filipinos were not rushing home. Letters from relatives and friends had given them a dismal picture of life back in the Philippines. They knew there were no jobs waiting for them there. Even more important, their sense of pride would not let them go back to the Philippines in defeat. To be transported home at public expense would be too humiliating. They were ashamed to go home without the riches they had expected to earn, unwilling to show themselves to their families once again unless they could sail to the Philippines with money in their pockets. One of the few Filipinos who returned to the islands under the Repatriation Act realized too late that he had made a mistake. "I have come home as a repatriate," he said sadly, "and that alone has given my name the stigma of failure as an adventurer."

The Filipinos had left the Philippines because they had found themselves facing grim futures in the islands. Some of them had left wives and children behind, planning to return. In a letter to his wife, a Filipino man in the United States wrote that he was "working steady from sunrise to sunset, six days a week. . . . If I can keep up with the hard work, God willing, I should be returning home in two years. . . . Enclosed is a small amount of $45.00. Set aside part of it for Antonio's education, and keep paying Tata Iniong for that piece of land where someday, we will build our own house."

The songs of the immigrants told of the sadness of such separations:

I promised it'll be a short
while perhaps
And I will be back home
It's been only three months
Since then
To me, it means
Three full years
And I count
Even the hours
Because the heart
Is filled with ache.

But four-fifths of the Filipinos who left their homes to seek prosperity in America never returned. "If I had enough money, by golly! I'd go home," one immigrant said. "I've been here 16 years and have saved nothing." Struggling for survival,

Filipinos were forced to drift along, carried by the currents of the Great Depression. "For nine months the Filipino Social Relief Service in Los Angeles had been giving a free meal every Sunday to the unemployed Filipinos," said the *Filipino Nation,* a Filipino newspaper in Los Angeles, in 1932. "So many came—often as many as 300 in one day. . . . Walk down First Street or enter any of the Filipino pool halls and, if you are a Filipino, you will immediately be surrounded by a large number of your countrymen begging for a dime or a nickel for something to eat."

The economic depression had trapped Filipinos in the United States. One of them wrote to his family in the Philippines, "We do not see any possibility at all of coming home. This depression has turned everything topsy-turvy. Wages are cut 70%. I have been out of work half of the time this year." Another reflected, "I wanted to go back to the Philippines, to serve my country and my people as a teacher. But the Depression put the fire out of me so I stayed on, and on, and on." One Filipino in California told his younger brother, "You shouldn't have come to America. But you can't go back now. You can never go back, Allos."

During the early years, there were few women and families in Filipino America. Many of the immigrants lived in temporary labor camps, with no chance to put down roots.

Chapter Four

The Filipino World in America

A UNIQUE FILIPINO WORLD EMERGED AMONG THE immigrants in America. They had grown up on the farms and in the villages of the Philippines, where traditions were strong and communities were stable. Now they found themselves moving from camp to camp, cut off from the mainstream of American society by prejudice and rivalry, with no chance to put down roots.

Unlike the Chinese with their Chinatowns and the Japanese with their Little Tokyos, the Filipinos did not develop their own neighborhoods in American cities. The Filipino districts in Stockton and Los Angeles were mainly gathering centers for migratory workers. They were not places to live and build long-term communities. Chinese and Japanese immigrants had started hundreds of businesses, but Filipinos did not open their own shops and grocery stores. In 1923, there was only one Filipino grocery store in Los Angeles; 20 years later, there were still only six. When Filipinos did open businesses, they provided services rather than goods. Filipinos were much more likely to own their own restaurants and barbershops than stores or trading companies.

The absence of Filipino merchants in America was partly the result of centuries of Spanish colonialism in the Philippines. Spanish officials in the Philippines had used the Philippines as a trading post, shipping silks, pottery, and other goods from China to Spain's colony in Mexico in exchange for Mexican gold and silver. The Spanish did not develop the local economy of the Philippines; instead, they allowed Chinese merchants to operate stores. Thus, the Filipinos who came to America did not have much experience in trade, shopkeeping, or banking. They arrived in the United States to find that earlier waves of Chinese and Japanese immigrants had already started businesses in American communities. These Chinese and Japanese stores served the needs of the Filipino immigrants, so there was little or no opportunity for Filipinos to open their own businesses. In addition, Filipinos arrived in the United States at the beginning of the Great Depression, a bad time to start new business ventures. Finally, unlike the Chinese and Japanese immigrants, most Filipinos could speak some English, which made it easier for them to get jobs as laborers. Chinese and Japanese immigrants were driven to create their own ethnic economies by the language barrier, but Filipinos did not face that obstacle.

Another reason why the Filipinos did not form ethnic neighborhoods and businesses was their way of life. Their work required them to be transient, always moving around with no fixed homes. Most of them were single men who worked as migratory workers, shuttling back and forth from Seattle and San Francisco to Alaska, or traveling constantly to work the fields in Washington, Oregon, and California.

More than the immigrants from China and Japan, Filipinos saw themselves as temporary visitors. They were from an American territory and thought they could come and go between the islands and the mainland as they pleased. Young Filipinos saw themselves as Americans "born under the Stars and Stripes," observed the Los Angeles newspaper *Filipino Nation* in 1931. As temporary sojourners on the American mainland, they felt little pressure to bring their families and cultural institutions to America in order to start businesses or to form communities.

The 1934 Tydings-McDuffie Act was another setback to the growth of Filipino communities in America because it cut off Filipino immigrants from their families in the Philippines. Wives and children could not come to the United States to join their husbands and fathers. The Filipino exclusion law was even more severe than the restrictions on Chinese and Japanese immigration. The Chinese exclusion law of 1882 had allowed Chinese merchants to bring their wives to America, and the Japanese exclusion law of 1908 had permitted family members to join immigrants as well. But the Tydings-McDuffie Act did not contain provisions for wives or family members to enter the United States. The only way for an immigrant man to see his family again was for him to go back to the Philippines.

Rootless and lonely, most Filipino farm laborers went into town on weekends. "After being in the camp for a long time you go wild the first few days in the city," said Felix Tapiz. "We congregated in Chinatown." Filipinos hunted for excitement in gambling joints and dance halls. Or they loitered on the streets in front of the Filipino barbershop, where they could sit around and share stories. Or they hung out in the pool halls, a popular pastime. For many of the Filipinos, the pool hall was "their world."

In the Chinatowns and in the camps, gambling was a favorite pastime. "Most of these boys never gambled once or even knew what it was until they came here," a Filipino told an interviewer in 1930. "But, you see, there are few amusements open to them here." After work, sitting on blankets, they played poker and blackjack until late at night. They also gathered at cockfights, watching two roosters engage in bloody combat. The audiences were swept away by the excitement and the flurry of violence, the betting, and the exchange of money. Recalled one immigrant, "Cockfights in Stockton was number one. Everybody used to love to go to the cock-

Maria Abastilla Beltran (left), one of the comparatively few Filipino women who emigrated from the islands, was a nurse in the Philippine Red Cross before coming to the United States to finish her education.

fights. . . . We used to do it in secret places. If we have fifty or one hundred Filipinos getting together, that's a good crowd for cockfighting."

On weekends, especially after payday, Filipinos crowded into gambling houses, which they called *sikoy-sikoy.* Here many of them lost not only the money they had earned that day but also their wages for the next few weeks and even months. "You work for one whole week, you go to the gambling house. You lose it all in one hour. Come Monday, you'll start all over again," said a Filipino. "Work, save your money, go to the gambling house on Saturday, lose your money, in sikoy-sikoy." An unlucky Filipino said regretfully, "There were too many gambling houses. Sometimes I lost what I earned . . . eighty dollars, fifty dollars. . . . lost everything."

Living in a world of men, far away from home and lacking the normal company of women, some migrants spent their money on prostitutes. Sometimes the women were delivered to the camps by taxi. Prostitutes "followed the seasons," a farm laborer stated, "the way Filipinos follow the crops."

One of the Filipinos' most popular pastimes was the dance hall. They flocked to dance halls with names like Pig and Whistle, Hippodrome, Mardong, Dreamland Saloon, Royal Palais, and Rizal Cabaret. There they danced to songs like "I Like Your Size, I Like Your Eyes," "Honey Bunch, You Know How Much I Love You," and "I Wish I Had My Old Girl Back Again." Filipino bands played lively music for favorite dances like the waltz, fox-trot, and polka. One band, the Manila Serenaders, was an 18-piece orchestra. Carlos Malla, a member of the band, recalled that they "played in

The staff of the Filipino Forum, *a monthly newspaper published in Seattle. Such papers helped forge a sense of community among Filipino Americans.*

Oregon, Idaho, all middle states going up as far as North Dakota and then South." Sometimes 500 or 1,000 people would crowd the ballrooms when the Manila Serenaders played.

"Bahala na," Filipino men shouted, meaning, "Come what may!" The dance hall was the place where they went to have a good time, to forget their problems. They spared no pains to look their best, dabbing themselves with cologne, slicking down their jet-black hair with sticky gel, and wearing fasionable suits—"sometimes white with padded shoulders, like suits Hollywood actors wear." Recalling those carefree times, Frank Coloma said, "There were four main dancing cabarets in Los Angeles and I had a girlfriend in every hall. I usually went there after going to the pool halls or gambling places, and I always wore the very best suit."

In the glittering dance hall, with pulsating music filling the night air, Filipino men were able to escape from the boredom and misery of their daily existence. There they could meet women, who worked as dance hostesses. "The girls were always Americans, mostly blondes," said a Filipino, "and you couldn't dance with them without money." In the dance halls, the hostesses told the men, "No money, no honey." The men could buy tickets to dance with the hostesses—a dime a dance, a 10-cent ticket for one minute of dancing. The men would buy rolls of tickets. "Most of the dime-a-dance halls had several dozen girls working there," a Filipino remembered. "Each dance cost a dime and was very short. Most of the boys bought a dollar's worth of dances."

On the dance floor, a man could spend a whole day's wages in 10 or 20 minutes. Many men went to the dance halls trying to buy love, only to find their hearts broken and their pockets empty. A Filipino told his sad story:

> My friend took me to the dance hall one night and there I met a beautiful girl. I fell in love with her. Night after night after finishing my work I could not help but go out to see her, and dance with her. For a while we were both very serious with one another. She finally asked me if I would marry her, and I consented to it, having spent a large sum of money for her already. [Then the man's boss fired him and hired someone else.] My girl friend felt that because of this sudden change I wasn't quite so generous to her as before, so she turned me down. Now all the money that I have been saving for years is all gone. My friends have deserted me. Now I am nothing but a helpless beggar.

The loneliness of Filipino men and their craving for the company of women often bordered on desperation. "We would not have led miserable lives, nor drifted from one shoulder to another, if, in the beginning, our women had come with us," an immigrant said. "We saw no point in growing roots—in making a home for ourselves." In 1930, four-fifths of the Filipino men in California were under 30 years of age and unmarried. Few of them would be able to marry Filipino women, for there was only 1 Filipino woman to every 14 men.

One man wrote to his aunt in the Philippines, asking her to find a wife for him: "Two days ago I received your most loving letter. . . . Tia [auntie], why take so long a time to find a girl for me. Remember, I am not particular. As long as that dear one has a bit of everything (you know what I mean) that will serve the partnership. Have you anyone in mind?"

The few Filipino women in America always attracted a lot of attention from the Filipino men. "Back in the 1920s, there weren't that many Filipinas," recalled one immigrant, adding that regardless of her looks or her age, every Filipino woman was "a queen." Camila Carido smiled as she described the attention she received from the Filipino men when she was a teenager during the 1920s: "We were treated like actresses. The men treated us like royalty. It didn't matter what you looked like. Just that we were Filipinas." Another Filipino woman had no trouble getting dates in Seattle. "I could date anyone," she said. "There were over one thousand five hundred Filipinos here. Imagine, they're all men." A popular song described the Filipina:

The Filipino woman
Like a star in the morning
To see her brings joy
There is a radiance
And great beauty.

But Filipino women, like the men, generally had to work. They cleaned homes as maids, harvested vegetables and fruit in the fields, or cooked for the work crews. "My recollections of my mother," an immigrant's daughter said, "are those of her working so hard in the kitchen. She not only did the cooking for camp and family, she also worked in the fields." A visitor to a ranch in 1930 noticed three Filipino women workers, dressed in men's clothes and paid the same wages as the men.

Although they were few in number, women immigrants helped to bring Filipino culture to the United States, introducing folk dances and foods. One woman made Filipino rice cakes for her children to sell.

But there were too few Filipinas for the Filipino men. Many of the men married Mexican, Chinese, Japanese, Alas-

An immigrant and her American-born daughters, photographed in California in 1929. Women like these led the way in preserving Filipino cultural traditions in the United States.

kan, or white women. "If there were Filipino women here," commented a Filipino labor contractor in 1930, "I am sure that Filipinos would not seek white girls." Another immigrant explained that "there weren't many Filipino women," and so the men married "white girls or Mexican girls." Most mixed couples in Los Angeles were Filipino-Mexican. A popular song was "Mexicali Rose I Love You." Filipino men found they had much in common with Mexican women. They shared the Spanish language and the Catholic faith. Filipino men could also take Mexican women to public places without getting the curious and hostile glances that they always received when they were with white women.

Unlike Chinese and Japanese men, many Filipino men dated and married white women. Filipino men did not have cultural barriers against marrying outside their own ethnic group. They had come from a society where persons of mixed ancestry were numerous and socially accepted. Filipino men also found it easier than most other Asian immigrants to meet and mingle with white women. They were familiar with Western culture because their homeland had long been under Spanish and then American domination. Educated in American schools and able to speak English to some extent, Filipino men saw themselves as Americans rather than foreigners. They felt natural and comfortable meeting white American women. In addition, they entered American society during the 1920s, when women were beginning to have more freedom from traditional restrictions. It began to be acceptable for young women to go to dance halls and other places where Filipino men and white women could meet and socialize.

Filipino men and white women who wished to marry encountered laws against racial intermarriage, especially in states such as Oregon and California. Couples had to travel to states that did not have such laws. "Intermarriage was not permitted in Portland [Oregon]," said one man. "We went to Washington where they allowed intermarriages." White women who married Filipinos became targets of discrimination. In 1930, in a case involving a German immigrant woman who was married to a Filipino man, a superior court judge in California ruled that white immigrant women who married Filipinos could not become naturalized citizens of the United States. A federal official went even further, stating that American women who married Filipinos would lose their U.S. citizenship.

Filipino-white couples became social outcasts. In restaurants, they often overheard hostile remarks. The owner of the Manila Pool Hall in San Jose, California, told an interviewer in 1930: "I have advised the boys against being seen with white girls in public. This is one of the quickest ways to cause trouble. . . . I have a friend who is married to a white girl, and they never dare to go out together."

"Even walking down the street with Filipino people," said a white woman who had married a Filipino man, "you received comments, thrown at you more or less." The comments were crude and insulting, based on racial prejudice. "It was just as low as you can get," said another Filipino man's white wife. "My neighbors said all kinds of rude things to my mother. I realize now that she suffered a lot on account of me, of us. I cried bushels of tears." Many white wives tried to avoid being seen in public with their Filipino husbands. The child of an interracial couple later recalled, "My mother, who is white, seemed reluctant to go out with my father or as a family group."

Some Filipino immigrants found jobs in the timber industry of Washington State.

Filipino men and white women had to overcome cultural differences in their marriages. Filipino men often felt out of place in their wives' social circles. "When among my wife's American friends I cannot make myself feel a part of the group," a Filipino man said. "At times I am reluctant to talk, because of my peculiar accent. This makes me appear inferior. . . . I can also feel their [coldness toward me.]" Their wives, in turn, experienced awkward moments in the company of Filipino friends. "When my husband's friends speak in their dialect," an American wife recounted, "I listen to them with eagerness, trying to grasp the nature of their conversation. When the group laughs, I also 'giggle' with them just to make them feel that I am really a 'makabayan,' [a member of the group]."

Gradually, a second generation began to emerge. By the 1940s, for example, there were about 500 Filipino and

Aside from agriculture, the biggest area of employment for Filipinos in the 1930s was in service jobs as bartenders, waiters, or gardeners.

part-Filipino children in Stockton, California. More than half of the children of Filipino immigrants were of mixed race. But whatever their racial heritage, the second-generation Filipino Americans grew up in a world of prejudice. They were frequently insulted with racial slurs by white children. They were viewed as foreigners, even though they had been born in America and were U.S. citizens.

Born in 1931, Liz Megino grew up in a white community in Oakland, California. "The students in the school I attended were white," she remembered. "I had many white friends but I never got invited to their parties." Another second-generation Filipino American said, "When I was in seventh or eighth grade we went to a certain park in Stockton to play. And I remember some children screaming and yelling at us, 'Go back to where you come from. Go back to the country you come from. You don't belong here.'" But the Filipino American children had been born in America.

Most children had little time to go to the park, however, for they had to work. "I was nine years old," recalled Josephine Romero Loable. "I started washing clothes and taking care of other little things that my mother couldn't do because she worked." Terry Rosal said, "Well, I really didn't have too much of a teenage life because, when I was fourteen, probably thirteen, I had to quit school. I had to go out in the fields and work. I worked on the asparagus farms as a cutter, as a shed boy, as a washer in the packing house." Stung by prejudice and saddled with work responsibilities, these children often drew strength and comfort from their *compadres*—their godparents. "I have two godparents," said Ignacio Ladrido Balaba. "When my mother died, love was extended from these two families." And Filipino children were also surrounded by their parents' friends, the host of Filipino men who did not find wives. These unmarried men were "uncles" to the children of the Filipino community in America, a community that was still struggling to make a place for itself in American society.

Carlos Bulosan became not only the voice of Filipino America but also a spokesman for all of America's poor and downtrodden.

Chapter Five

An Immigrant's Dreams

FILIPINO AMERICA FOUND A VOICE IN CARLOS BULOSAN who was born the son of a farmer in Binalonan on the Philippine island of Luzon. When he arrived in America in 1930, Bulosan was only a boy, just 17 years old. He had promised his family, "I will come back someday." Bulosan never returned to the Philippines, yet he never became an American citizen. "I know deep down in my heart," he wrote to a friend, "that I am an exile in America."

Like most of his fellow Filipinos, Bulosan was a cannery worker, dishwasher, houseboy, and farm laborer. "Do you know what a Filipino feels in America?" he asked. In his book *America Is in the Heart: A Personal History,* published in 1946, he described the feelings of many Filipinos. To write the book, Bulosan drew deeply on his own experiences and those of the Filipinos around him to create a moving and powerful story that captures the reality of Filipino America.

Bulosan had journeyed to America in his mind long before he had actually stepped from the ship in Seattle. By the time he was born, the Philippines had been a colony of the United States for 15 years. Under American rule, public education was spreading through the islands, introducing ideas of opportunity and democracy. As a young boy, Bulosan felt the excitement of these new ideas. One of his older brothers came home one day with a book filled with pictures and large letters. "If you learn to read this book," Amado told Carlos, "I will take you to school with me." Carlos replied boastfully, "I will learn to read it in one day."

Years later Carlos Bulosan would remember how he had been moved by Amado's promise: "His words seized my mind and nourished my life to the edge of the day. I was greatly fascinated with the idea of going to school, but did not know why, since there was no hope of my going beyond the third grade." What Carlos and other Filipino children learned in school seemed to contradict what was happening to Filipino farmers and peasants. In school they learned about "ideas of social equality and of justice before the law," but at home they watched their parents lose their farms to distant, faceless landlords.

As a boy in the Philippines, Carlos encountered American people and products in the streets and marketplaces. American businessmen had begun moving to the Philippines, living in "beautiful white houses" high in the hills. American tourists crowded the markets, eagerly taking pictures of scantily clad, rural Filipinos. One day in the marketplace, Carlos was given ten centavos by an American lady tourist for undressing before her camera. "I had found," he said later, "a simple way to make a living."

Another American woman opened Carlos's eyes in a different way. He met her when she asked him to carry her groceries to her home in a wheelbarrow. "I will never forget Miss Mary Strandon on the day I pushed the wheelbarrow to her apartment," he said. "When I had carefully piled the vegetables and rice in the kitchen, she opened her purse and offered me five centavos." Noticing the dirt on his face, she told him to wash his face and gave him a bar of soap to use—it was the first time he had ever used soap. Mary Strandon, a librarian, hired Carlos as a houseboy to cook dinner and clean her house. During his free time, Carlos visited a houseboy who was working for another American woman who lived nearby. The two boys talked about their plans to go to America. They studied English, reading books about the country of their dreams. One of the stories they read was about Abraham Lincoln. "Who *is* this Abraham Lincoln?" Carlos asked his friend. The other answered, "He was a poor boy who became a president of the United States. He was born in a log cabin and walked miles and miles to borrow a book so that he would know more about his country."

Fascinated by the story, Carlos told Strandon about what he had been reading and asked her to tell him more about Lincoln. "I didn't know you could read," she said, and then she described the great man who had freed the black slaves. From that day on, "this poor boy who became president" filled the thoughts of young Carlos Bulosan. His employer brought him books from the library and helped to open "a whole new world" to the boy from Binalonan.

But his reading and his dreams had not prepared him for his experiences in America. When Bulosan arrived in Seattle, he had only 20 cents. He was able to hitch a ride with four other Filipinos to a hotel on King Street, "the heart of Filipino life in Seattle." The hotel keeper glanced at their suitcases and asked for the rent.

"We have no money, sir," Bulosan admitted politely.

"That is too bad," the man muttered. He walked outside, returning with "a short, fat Filipino," who looked at the young men "stupidly with his dull, small eyes, and spat his cigar out of the window." He pulled a fat roll of bills from his pocket, giving $25 to the hotel keeper, and shouted, "You are working for me now. Get your hats and follow me." In this way, Carlos and the others were "sold for five dollars each to work in the fish canneries of Alaska." They were forced to sign a paper that stated that each owed the labor contractor

$20 for bedding and another $20 for "luxuries." "What the luxuries were," Bulosan remarked later, "I have never found out."

Shipped to Alaska, Bulosan and his four companions joined the thousands of Filipinos who lived in bunkhouses unfit for human habitation and worked for the fishing industry. The canneries were dark and smelly. The work was exhausting and dangerous. Bulosan was assigned to a job rinsing beheaded fish that came down a small escalator. There he witnessed a horrifying incident: "One afternoon a cutter above me, working in the poor light, slashed off his right arm with the cutting machine. It happened so swiftly he did not cry out. I saw his arm floating down the water among the fish heads."

When the season was over, Bulosan returned to Seattle, where he was paid. The labor contractor handed him a slip of paper, and he was amazed at the neatly itemized list of charges he had supposedly accrued in Alaska: $100 for room and board, $20 for bedding, and so on. After these "expenses" were subtracted, his take-home pay for the whole hard season turned out to be only $13.

So began Bulosan's sojourn in America. After his stint in Alaska, he drifted from job to job, from unemployment line to unemployment line. He had entered the America of the Great Depression. Jobs were scarce and wages were low. Like many Filipino farm laborers, Bulosan followed the crops. He picked apples in the Yakima Valley of Washington; next, he went down to California to harvest winter peas in Holtville and pick oranges in Riverside. He rode a freight train to Idaho to pick peas and then another train to Montana where "the beet season was in full swing. Mexicans from Texas and New

Workers gather to receive their assignments from a labor contractor. Upon arriving in America, Bulosan fell into the hands of such a contractor, who shipped him to Alaska.

Mexico were everywhere; their jalopies dotted the highways. There were also Filipinos from California and Washington. Some of them had just come back from the fish canneries in Alaska." Bulosan rode the rails again: back to Seattle, then through Oregon to California, where he joined a crew that was planting cauliflower.

He found himself in Lompoc, California, when winter set in. It was cold in Lompoc, for the winter wind was beginning to invade the valley from the ocean. "The lettuce heads were heavy with frost," said Bulosan. "I worked with thick cotton gloves and a short knife. When the lettuce season was over the winter peas came next. I squatted between the long rows of peas and picked with both hands, putting the pods in a large petroleum can that I dragged with me." Bulosan sometimes worked as a dishwasher and a houseboy, and he did odd jobs here and there. Desperation and hunger drove him to extremes. Once he used a gun to rob a Japanese man. Another time he stole a diamond ring from a house while a woman was upstairs taking a bath.

Bulosan began to understand how Filipinos in America felt. Treated as inferior, they had created "a wall around themselves in their little world, and what they did behind it was theirs alone." After the long work week in the fields, they retreated to Chinatowns in cities like Stockton and Seattle. There, "waiting for the night," hundreds of "Filipinos in magnificent suits" stood in front of poolrooms, gambling houses, and dance halls. Bulosan remembered the first time he went to a dance hall:

> I came to a building which brightly dressed white women were entering, lifting their diaphanous gowns as they climbed the stairs. I looked up and saw the huge sign: MANILA DANCE HALL. The orchestra upstairs was playing; Filipinos were entering. I put my hands in my pockets and followed them, beginning to feel lonely for the sound of home.
>
> The dance hall was crowded with Filipino cannery workers and domestic servants. But the girls were very few, and the Filipinos fought over them. When a boy liked a girl he bought a roll of tickets from the hawker on the floor and kept dancing with her. . . . [My friend Marcelo] was dancing with a tall blonde in a green dress, a girl so tall that Marcelo looked like a dwarf climbing a tree. But the girl was pretty and her body was nicely curved and graceful, and she had a way of swaying that aroused confused sensations in me. . . . [Marcelo had a roll of tickets],

and the girl was supposed to tear off one ticket every three minutes, but I noticed that she tore off a ticket for every minute. That was ten cents a minute.

But every minute seemed worth it, helping Filipinos forget the humiliations, abuse, and racial attacks. Bulosan saw how Filipinos were forced to live in the worst parts of town, unable to rent rooms in good neighborhoods. In Los Angeles, Bulosan and his brother Macario lived in a wild and lawless district. Their room was on Hope Street, but Bulosan explained that the character of the street did not match its name: "It was a noisy and tragic street, where suicides and murders were a daily occurence, but it was the only place in the city were we could find a room. There was no other district where we were allowed to reside." When they tried to rent an apartment in the Vermont Avenue neighborhood, they saw a landlady take down her For Rent sign as they approached, and

Packing cans of Alaskan salmon, 1938.

they were told directly by another landlady, "We don't take Filipinos!" Feeling excluded and bitter, Bulosan's brother said, "Well, there is nothing else to do but go back to *our* world."

Bulosan witnessed and experienced racial discrimination. Once in a small town he saw a Filipino come into town with his white wife and their child. The couple entered a little restaurant and sat down at a table. No one would serve them, so they left. Outside the child began to cry. The Filipino father returned to the restaurant, asking to buy a bottle of milk for the baby. "For *your* baby?" the owner shouted, coming out from behind the counter.

"Yes, sir," replied the Filipino.

"You goddamn brown monkeys have your nerve, marrying our women. Now get out of this town!" the man yelled as he punched the Filipino between the eyes.

In San Diego, Bulosan was turned away from hotels and refused service at a lunch counter. In San Fernando, a citrus-growing community near Los Angeles, a Filipino labor contractor, who had planted lemon trees and helped to turn the valley into farmland, told Bulosan, "I have made this valley fruitful and famous. Some ten years ago I wanted to go into farming myself, so close I was to the soil, so familiar with the touch of clay and loam. But I found that I couldn't buy land in California." When he was ill in the Los Angeles County Hospital, Bulosan was told by a social worker, "You Filipinos ought to be shipped back to your jungle homes."

At a farm in the Yakima Valley of Washington, Bulosan and his fellow Filipino farm laborers were driven into the darkness by white men shooting guns and brandishing clubs. In Klamath Falls, Oregon, Bulosan was arrested by two policemen who called him a "brown monkey," robbed him of his $2, brutally beat him, and marched him to the California border. On another occasion, Bulosan and a Filipino friend were trying to organize farm laborers in Salinas, California. They were in the back room of a restaurant, writing a leaflet to be circulated among the workers, when five white men kidnapped them at gunpoint. In the dark night they were driven across a beet field to some woods; there they were stripped naked, tarred and feathered, and viciously punched and kicked repeatedly. "The man on my right got out [of the car] and pulled me violently after him, hitting me on the jaw," Bulosan recounted. "Blood came out of my mouth. I raised my hand to wipe it off, but my attacker hit me again."

But while America could be cruel, Bulosan knew that it could also be kind. Once, for example, he and some friends were trying to run away from white detectives in a railroad yard. His friend Jose fell, and one of his legs was amputated by the wheels of a moving train car. They carried Jose to the highway, seeking help, but the passing motorists looked scornfully and spat at them. Finally an old man came along in a truck and drove them to the county hospital, where a kind doctor and two nurses did their best for Jose. "Walking down the marble stairway of the hospital," Bulosan began "to wonder at the paradox of America."

The paradox puzzled and intrigued Bulosan. How could America be so cruel and at the same time so kind? In his search for answers, he thought about the white women he had come to know. One of them was Helen, a labor organizer he met during a farm laborers' strike. From the very beginning, he was suspicious of her, noting how she used her "womanly ways" to attract and influence the strike leaders. At her suggestion, the strikers decided to block the trucks that

A Filipino band. Bulosan saw that his fellow Filipinos, rejected by the larger society, sought comfort in "their little world" of dance halls and pool rooms.

carried the lettuce from the fields. Helen's plan turned out to be a setup. When the strikers tried to stop the trucks, they were clubbed and beaten, and their leaders were arrested. Helen disappeared, and Bulosan later learned that she was a professional strikebreaker, paid to undermine the labor movement. When Bulosan and a friend caught up with Helen in Los Angeles, she exclaimed angrily, "I hate Filipinos as deeply as I hate unions! You are all savages and you have no right to stay in this country!"

Helen represented America's mean and exclusionist spirit. But other white women expressed America's sympathy and kindness. After Bulosan escaped from the white thugs in Salinas, he found refuge in the home of a white woman named Marian. "What was the matter with this land?" he asked, confused. "Just a moment ago I was being beaten by white men. But here was another white person, a woman, giving me food and a place to rest. And her warmth! I sat on the couch and started talking. I wanted to explain what happened to me." Marian made Bulosan's heart ache, for "this woman was like my little sisters in Binalonan. I turned away from her, remembering how I had walked familiar roads with my mother." She drove Bulosan to Los Angeles where she gave him some money, saying, "Now you can go to the university." Marian died shortly afterward. "She was," Bulosan said lovingly, "the song of my dark hour."

On another occasion, Bulosan befriended a homeless young woman named Mary. "Her hair was light brown, her skin milk-white. But her eyes were deep blue and frightened." Mary became a member of the household, cooking for Bulosan and his friends. She became a "symbol of goodness" and "purity," their "hope for a better America." Another woman friend was Eileen Odell, who visited Bulosan in the hospital, bringing flowers and paper sacks full of delicacies. For Bulosan, Eileen was "undeniably the *America*" he had wanted to find in those "frantic days of fear and flight, in those acute hours of hunger and loneliness. This America was human, good, and real."

As he traveled around the country looking for the America that people like Eileen represented, Bulosan found his heart going out not only to his poor fellow Filipinos but also to others in poverty and trouble. Riding in a boxcar with a group of hobos, Bulosan kept staring at a young African American. It was the first time that he had ever seen a black person. "Where are you going, boy?" the African American asked Bulosan.

"California, sir," Bulosan answered.

"Sir?" the young African American laughed. "Boy, you are far from California!" Bulosan began to understand how it felt to be black in America.

In Montana, Bulosan met a Jewish girl in a drugstore. Later he remembered what she had said: "It is hard to be a Jew!" When he was in the hospital, he became acquainted with a "poor American boy" from Arkansas who had "never learned to write." Slowly, Bulosan grew to understand what his brother Macario had told him:

> America is not a land of one race or one class of men. We are all Americans that have toiled and suffered and known oppression and defeat, from the first Indian that offered peace in Manhattan to the last Filipino pea pickers. . . . America is also the nameless foreigner, the homeless refugee, the hungry boy begging for a job and the black body dangling on a tree. America is the illiterate immigrant who is ashamed that the world of books and intellectual opportunities is closed to him.

For Bulosan, the task was not only to understand America but also to make it into a just society. He wanted the America of his dreams to become a reality. There had been moments when Bulosan felt like lashing out violently against a cruel America. On one occasion two policemen, waving pistols, invaded a party at a Filipino restaurant and physically abused Bulosan, his friends, and their honored guest—a prominent educator from the Philippines. "I felt violated and outraged," said Bulosan. He thought of his gun lying on the table of his room, and after the policemen left the restaurant, Bulosan rushed outside, running blindly toward his hotel. "I wanted my gun. With it I could challenge our common enemy bullet for bullet. It seemed my only friend and comfort in this alien country—this smooth little bit of metal." In the hotel room, his brother Macario grabbed the gun from him. Collapsing in rage on his bed, Bulosan lay face down, holding his chest against the "wild beating" of his heart. He made a vow:

He would strike back, but not with bullets. Words would become his weapon.

Writing, Bulosan understood, could be a political act. Even as a young boy in the Philippines, he had been encouraged by his brother Luciano to become a writer, wielding his pen for the people. In a discussion on politics, Luciano had told Carlos, "You must never stop reading good books. . . . Reading is food for the mind. Healthy ideas are food for the mind. Maybe someday you will be a journalist." Carlos wondered: *Journalist!* What did it mean? Many years later, lying in total darkness in a hospital in America, Bulosan remembered the hardships of his parents and the other poverty-stricken

Bulosan helped organize farm workers' strikes. He realized that workers of all colors and nationalities had more in common than they thought, and he wanted to help awaken a feeling of unity among them.

peasants in the Philippines and sobbed, "Yes, I will be a writer and make all of you live again in my words."

Bulosan turned to the writers of his own time for strength. He found Younghill Kang, a writer who had immigrated to the United States from Korea when he was a boy. Kang's "indomitable courage" rekindled in Bulosan "a fire of hope." Earlier, Bulosan had met a hopeful young Filipino writer named Estevan. Sickly and starving, Estevan declared, "I haven't become a writer in America in vain. Someday, my friends, I will write a great book about the Ilocano peasants in northern Luzon." Estevan had written stories and essays, but none of them had been published. Still, he had impressed Bulosan, who said, "He was the first writer I knew. . . . Thus it was that I began to rediscover my native land, and the cultural roots there that had nourished me, and I felt a great urge to identify myself with the social awakening of my people."

The urge to write sprang from rage. It expressed itself suddenly one day in a hotel room in San Luis Obispo, California. Bulosan had started writing a letter to his brother Macario, when he realized suddenly, "like a revelation," that he could "actually write understandable English." Swept away by the thrill of this discovery, Bulosan felt powerful. He wrote all night. When he finished his long letter, which was a story of his life, he had jumped to his feet and shouted joyously through his tears, "They can't silence me any more! I'll tell the world what they have done to me!"

The next day Bulosan met Pascal, the editor of a workers' newspaper. Bulosan saw that the farm workers were "voiceless," and he decided to become their voice. He wrote many pages for Pascal, seeking to tell the world about the suffering, the hard work, and the political struggles of the laborers in the fields. "That's it, Carl," Pascal would shout, encouragingly. "Write your guts out! Write with thunder and blood!"

In his development as a writer and thinker, Bulosan was also greatly influenced by several white women. While he was working as a dishwasher at a hotel, Bulosan met Judith, who worked in a grocery store across the street. She had brown hair and blue eyes, and he would go to the store "pretending to buy something," but he "wanted only to look at her." When she asked him what he wanted, he fumbled for something to say.

"Oh, you don't understand English well?" she said.

"No, ma'am," he replied.

"Oh, don't 'ma'am' me," she smiled. "I'm just a young girl. See? My name is Judith. I have some books. You'd like to read, perhaps?"

Bulosan followed her through the back door and up into a house. In the living room, he saw books of many sizes and colors piled along the wall; enchanted, he was irresistibly drawn toward them and was overjoyed when she offered to share her books with him. He recalled, "When my dishes were done, working faster, I ran to the store so Judith could read to me."

Bulosan also received encouragement from Dora Travers, a member of the Young Communist League. He wrote a poem about her and read it to her. "Write more poems, Carl," she said appreciatively. "I like your music. I think you will be a good *American* poet." Bulosan felt inspired.

There was "music" in him, "stirring to be born." That evening, he wrote far into the night. The words came to him effortlessly. He wrote 10 or 15 poems in one sitting. Bulosan felt that he "could fight the world now with [his] mind, not merely with [his] hands."

Besides Dora Travers and Judith, there were others. Harriet Monroe, editor of *Poetry: A Magazine of Verse,* noticed Bulosan's talent as a writer and began publishing his poems; she also offered to arrange a university scholarship for him. After reading Bulosan's poems, a writer named Alice Odell introduced herself to him. When Bulosan spent two years in the hospital being treated for tuberculosis, Alice and her sister Eileen visited him regularly. Alice read books to him, including Thomas Wolfe's *Look Homeward, Angel.* Eileen also gave him books and talked to him about them by the hour. When Bulosan became restless, he wrote letters to Eileen. Every day the words poured out of his pen. Bulosan began to "cultivate a taste for words, not so much for their meanings as their sounds and shapes." He tried to depend "only on the music of words" to express his ideas.

As a writer, Bulosan wanted to help Filipinos—"my own kind"— understand "this vast land" from their own experiences. In his work, he would "piece together the mosaic of [their] lives in America." Through his writing, he hoped to help not only other Filipinos but "all Americans" who had "toiled and suffered and known oppression and defeat." He wanted to show them what he had learned: They were all beaten down by the "same forces," and they were pitted against one another, so that they could be more easily exploited. Once while working on a farm, Bulosan had seen that Japanese workers were housed in another section of the farm.

Years later he discovered that the farmers kept the Filipino and Japanese workers apart so that the two groups would not join together to demand better wages and working conditions.

On another occasion, Bulosan helped organize a Filipino strike in the lettuce fields. He watched the growers bring in Mexican laborers to break the strike. During another strike, Bulosan noted that the Mexican and Filipino workers did not unite, even though, as Bulosan saw, there were cultural and economic ties between them. The workers had not yet recognized "one important point: that the beet companies conspired against their unity."

But the oppression of the workers, Bulosan saw, also taught them important lessons about the strength that they could find within themselves and in unity with one another. "Our awakening was spontaneous: it grew from our experiences and our responses to them," he said. In San Pedro, California, Bulosan attended a meeting of cannery workers—Japanese, Mexicans, Filipinos, and white Americans. They spoke out "in broken English, but always with sincerity and passion," making Bulosan hope that workers of all backgrounds could learn to understand one another. They were immigrants, but they knew that they were Americans, too, and had earned their right to claim their adopted country. Yet although they had toiled in its farms and its fisheries, America remained for them an unfinished dream, a society not yet willing to embrace its diversity.

When World War II broke out, Filipino Americans flocked to enter the U.S. armed forces. This 17-year-old Filipino boy, being given a flower by two Japanese American children, was a member of the Hawaiian Territorial Guard, hastily formed after the attack on Pearl Harbor.

Chapter Six

World War II and After

ONE SUNDAY AFTERNOON IN LOS ANGELES, WHILE HE was sitting in a bar, Carlos Bulosan was suddenly stunned by a blaring news announcement on the radio: "Japan bombs Pearl Harbor!" War had been raging in Asia as Japan sent troops into China, Korea, and Southeast Asia. The United States had stayed out of the war—but now Japan had attacked a U.S. naval base in Hawaii. Surely the United States would enter the conflict. What would happen to the Philippines?

Bulosan rushed outside, trembling and looking for a familiar face. "It has come, Carlos!" his brother Macario shouted. The two men walked aimlessly in the streets. Memories of home and fears about the future swept through Bulosan like waves. "We had been but little boys when we left the Philippines," he thought. "And my mother! What would happen to her and my two sisters?" A few months later, Macario joined the army. As he watched his brother ride away on the bus, Bulosan sensed that the war would have a profound effect on their lives and on American society. "If I met him again, I would not be the same," he thought. "He would not be the same, either. Our world was this one, but a new one was being born."

One Filipino woman never forgot the Japanese attack on Pearl Harbor. The Japanese planes swooped down on December 7, 1941, shattering the calm of this Sunday morning in Hawaii. "The airplanes looked like toys but they were shooting and dropping bombs on us," recalled Apolinaria Gusman Oclaray, who had left the Philippines with her husband in 1928. "I thought it was play, you know practice, and I asked my husband, 'How come the airplanes are firing?'

And he said, 'Because this is a real war and a real war is like that.'" Seven hours later, Japanese forces invaded the Philippine islands. The Philippines became the scene of some of the most bitter and important battles fought in the Pacific during World War II. On the Bataan peninsula of Luzon Island, the Japanese invaders met determined resistance from American and Filipino troops.

Four long months later, on April 9, 1942, a news correspondent described the fall of Bataan: "The gallant United States and Philippine forces in Bataan peninsula surrendered today after enduring the tortures of hell. . . . They were beaten, but it was a fight that ought to make every American bow his head in tribute. . . . The Americans fought for everything they loved, as did the Filipinos, WITH THEIR FIERCE LOVE OF LIBERTY."

In her tribute to the brave men of Bataan, Eleanor Roosevelt, the wife of President Franklin D. Roosevelt, spoke of the interracial brotherhood forged on the bloodstained battlefield. She said, "Fighting in Bataan has been an excellent example of what happens when two different races respect each other. Men of different races and backgrounds have fought side by side and praised each other's heroism and courage."

Carlos Bulosan conveyed in poetry the meaning of Bataan for Filipinos:

Bataan has fallen.
With heads bloody but unbowed, we yielded to the
enemy. . . .
We have stood up uncomplaining.
Besieged on land and blockaded by sea,

The Japanese attack on Pearl Harbor brought the United States into the war—and indirectly brought about a change in the fortunes of Filipino Americans.

We have done all that human endurance could
bear. . . .
Our defeat is our victory.

At Bataan thousands of Filipinos had fought beside American soldiers. Stories of Filipino military gallantry forced whites to view Filipinos in the United States more respectfully. Suddenly there was something "in the air," writer Manuel Buaken noticed, that said America had learned to respect Filipinos. "No longer on the streetcar do I feel myself in the presence of my enemies," he said. "We Filipinos are the same—it is Americans that have changed in their recognition of us." A Filipino working in a railroad car was pleasantly surprised by the abrupt change in the attitudes of white travelers. "I am very much embarrassed," he remarked. "They treat me as if I have just arrived from Bataan."

Meanwhile, Filipinos in America worried about the Philippines and the loved ones they had left behind. They wanted to defend their homeland, and they immediately rushed to the recruiting offices to volunteer for the armed forces. They were refused, however, for they were classified as "nationals," not citizens, which meant that they could not serve in the military. When he learned that his village of Binalonan had been crushed by Japanese tanks racing toward Manila, Bulosan went to the nearest recruiting office, hoping to sign up. Later he said, "As I stood in line waiting for my turn, I thought of a one-legged American Revolutionary patriot of whom I had read. But Filipinos were not being accepted."

The insignia of the First Filipino Infantry Regiment of the United States Army.

They had to get into this war, Filipinos insisted. President Franklin Roosevelt listened to their pleas and promptly changed the draft law so that Filipinos could join the armed forces. On February 19, 1942, the secretary of war announced the organization of the First Filipino Infantry Regiment: "This new unit is formed in recognition of the intense loyalty and patriotism of those Filipinos who are now residing in the United States. It provides for them a means of serving in the armed forces of the United States, and the eventual opportunity of fighting on the soil of their homeland."

Filipinos eagerly responded to the call to arms. In California alone, 16,000 men—two-fifths of the state's Filipino population—registered to enter the military. In 1942, the First Filipino Infantry Regiment and the Second Filipino Infantry Regiment were formed. More than 7,000 Filipinos served in these two regiments. "Their enthusiasm and discipline are far superior to any I have seen in my army career," declared their white commander. "The minute you put one of these boys in uniform he wants a rifle. The minute he gets a rifle he wants to get on a boat. He can't understand why we don't ship him out right away, so he can start [fighting]."

"To these pint-sized soldiers," stated the *American Legion Magazine* describing the Filipinos, "this war is a personal grudge." Filipino American soldiers had, as one of them said, "a personal reason to be training to fight the invaders." They wanted to defend their country. "My home and my family and all the things that were dear to me as a boy," explained Doroteo Vite in 1942, "are there in the path of the Japanese war machine." Another said that he met white men who were "thrilled" at the sight of Filipinos in America, admiring them as representatives of the people of the Philippines, who were putting up a fierce fight against the Japanese.

Filipinos in the United States were eager to get back to the Philippines to fight for the liberation of their homeland, which had fallen to Japan by May 1942. The Filipino Americans declared, "We want to be there"—in the Philippines. The regimental song of the First Filipino Infantry was "On to Bataan." Shipped to the Pacific for duty, the soldiers were anxious for action. "After we came from Australia by submarine we went to the Philippines," said one. "We trained in Australia under General MacArthur . . . learned how to roll parachutes, jump in combat . . . how to kill people noiselessly." Filipino soldiers made unique and valuable contributions to the war effort in the Pacific. They operated behind enemy lines, engaging in sabotage to destroy Japanese communications. The military information gathered by Filipino soldiers, reported a U.S. lieutenant general, proved to be "of the greatest assistance to impending military operations." He added, "By their loyalty, daring, and skillful performance of duty under hazardous conditions, they materially accelerated the campaign for the recapture of the Philippine Islands."

Many Filipino American soldiers also saw the war as a chance to fight for their freedom at home, in the United States. The fact that they could wear a soldier's uniform was a political statement. "In a few months I will be wearing Uncle Sam's olive-drab army uniform," said a Filipino. "I am looking forward to that day, not with misgiving but with a boyish anticipation of doing something which up to now I have never been allowed to do—serving as an equal with American boys." The wife of a Filipino soldier claimed that the war gave Filipinos the chance to show themselves to America as "soldiers of democracy," as "men, not houseboys."

To Filipinos, joining the army gave them membership in American society. "In all the years I was here before the United States went into the war," a Filipino soldier observed, "I felt that I did not belong here. I was a stranger among a people who did not understand and had no good reason to understand me and my people. . . . In other words, it was a pretty difficult business to be a Filipino in the United States in the years preceding Pearl Harbor."

But in many places it was still "difficult business" even after Pearl Harbor. Filipinos continued to be viewed as "strangers." Stationed at Camp Beale in California, soldiers of the First Filipino Infantry found they were unwelcome in the nearby town of Marysville. Dressed proudly in their U.S. Army uniforms, several Filipino soldiers went into town during their first weekend pass to have a good dinner and see the sights. They entered a restaurant and sat down, but no one came to serve them. After waiting for half an hour, one of them got up and asked for service. He was told, "We don't serve Filipinos here." Filipino soldiers were turned away from theaters or were forced to sit in a segregated section. Wives who visited them were refused rooms at the hotels.

When the colonel who commanded the regiment heard about the discriminatory treatment that his men were receiving, he met with the Marysville Chamber of Commerce. "There," said Manuel Buaken, a private in the regiment, "he laid down the law of cooperation with the army—or else. Then the merchants and the restaurant proprietors and the movie houses changed their tune," and opened their doors to Filipinos. But the "soul of enjoyment" was gone for Buaken and his brothers. They knew in their hearts that the merchants and waiters were hating and ridiculing the Filipinos, laughing at their brown skin. And the Filipino soldiers hoped that they would soon be gone from "these towns which hate built" and "this land of double-talk."

Slowly, however, the war began to open the way for Filipinos. Above all, it enabled many of them to claim citizenship. As members of the U.S. armed forces, they were allowed to become American citizens. On February 20, 1943, on the parade ground of Camp Beale, 1,200 Filipino soldiers stood proudly and silently in formation as citizenship was conferred on them. During the ceremony, their colonel said, "Officers who returned from Bataan have said there are no finer soldiers in the world than the Filipinos who fought and starved and died there shoulder to shoulder with our troops. I can well believe it as I look at the men before me. On those faces is quiet determination and a consciousness of training and discipline with a definite end in view. I congratulate them on their soldierly appearance and on their approaching citi-

The heroism of Filipino American soldiers was praised by their officers and comrades in arms.

zenship." In the concluding speech, a judge welcomed the Filipinos, saying, "Citizenship came to us who were born here as a heritage—it will come to you as a privilege. We have every faith you will become and remain loyal, devoted citizens of the United States."

During the war, the attorney general of California studied the state's land laws and decided that Filipinos could be allowed to lease land. He encouraged them to take over the land that had belonged to U.S. residents of Japanese descent, who had been interned in concentration camps during the war because it was thought that they might pose a threat to military security on the West Coast. Fearful of being mistaken for Japanese, Filipinos took pains to identify themselves. A Filipino woman recalled instructions from her mother shortly after the beginning of the war: "My mother told me to make sure you say you're not Japanese if they ask you who you are. Filipinos wore buttons saying, 'I am a Filipino.'"

Manuel Buaken welcomed the internment of the Japanese Americans and the changes in the laws that enabled Filipinos to become citizens and lease land. Buaken felt that the Japanese immigrants, by teaching their children Japanese and creating their own business communities, had shown that they were not really interested in becoming part of American society. Filipinos, however, were ready and eager to blend in, as Buaken explained: "We have always wanted nothing more than to learn from America, to become good Americans. We have developed no great banks here in the United States—our savings have gone into American banks. We have patronized American stores—not stores devoted to the selling of products from across the seas. We have striven to learn English, not to perpetuate foreign language schools and to teach foreign ideas to our children." Sadly, Buaken's ideas grew out of anti-Japanese feelings rather than America's democratic ideals.

These ideals had to be more sharply defined during the war. Fighting against dictatorship abroad, the United States felt that it must make good its claims to democracy. Some steps were taken toward equal rights. In 1941, Roosevelt issued an executive order that outlawed racial discrimination in the workplace. The order said, "It is the duty of employers and labor organizations . . . to provide for full and equitable participation of all workers in defense industries, without discrimination because of race, creed, color, or national origin." At the same time, new job opportunities opened for Filipinos because the war industries needed work-

A Filipino American air force sergeant stationed in England.

ers. The hiring of Filipinos in shipyards and munitions factories prompted one Filipino to remark shortly before he left to fight in the Pacific, "In the United States, the war is doing wonders for the resident Filipinos."

Soon after the war ended in 1945, the U.S. Congress passed a law that allowed Filipino immigrants to become citizens. "It took a war and a great calamity in our country to bring us [whites and Filipinos] together," observed Carlos Bulosan. The new law also increased the number of Filipino immigrants who could enter the United States each year from 50 to 100, which became the annual quota after the Philippines received full independence in 1946.

Meanwhile, a social scientist studied the way the war had changed the status of Filipinos. He noted that as the Japanese left Los Angeles, Filipinos bought homes from them in the more desirable neighborhoods. Many Filipinos also bought small farms from the Japanese in California's agricultural districts. Job opportunities expanded for Filipinos as they entered shipyards and manufacturing plants as welders, technicians, assembly or office workers, and, in a few cases, engineers. Above all, the sociologist observed, the war had forced Filipinos to make a decision—"to go home and help in the reconstruction of their homeland" or "to spend the rest of their days in America." Thousands of Filipinos, granted citizenship and feeling a sense of greater acceptance, chose to make America their permanent home. But would whites forget Bataan when the war faded from memory and economic growth slowed down, bringing hard times again? Would Filipino Americans be doomed to another "interminable era of dishwashing and asparagus cutting"?

Leaders of the anti-Japanese guerrilla forces in the battle to liberate the Philippines celebrate their merger with General Douglas MacArthur's troops.

Filipinos had reason to be doubtful. They had finally been granted citizenship, but they knew that their new status did not mean that white Americans truly accepted them. "What good would it do to become citizens of America," asked a Filipino soldier, "if we are still brown-skin inferiors?" Filipinos could not change their complexion. To some white people, they remained just "Orientals."

Even before the end of the war, Filipinos in California's Santa Maria Valley were reminded that they were not regarded as equals in society. After Filipino farm laborers went on strike, the Economic Council of Santa Maria warned that the wartime honeymoon for Filipinos was over: "At best, Filipinos are guests in the United States. . . ." Filipinos wondered whether they would ever be able to claim equality. Would they ever be seen as fellow Americans, as men and women who truly belonged in the United States, instead of as "guests"?

The election of Corazon Aquino to the presidency of the Philippines in 1986 inspired hopes that an era of democracy and reform had come to the island nation.

Chapter Seven

The Second Wave

IN THE YEARS AFTER WORLD WAR II, FILIPINOS CONTINued to immigrate to the United States, although only 100 could enter the country each year. Unlike the earlier wave of immigrants, those who came in the 1940s and 1950s included many women and children. The imbalance between men and women among the Filipino immigrant community changed. Once there had been dozens of men for every woman, but by 1963 there were only a little more than two men for every woman. Filipino American families became more common.

Despite the improved economic opportunities for Filipinos during the war, Filipinos generally still found themselves limited to jobs as field- or service workers. In 1950, more than half of all Filipino workers in California were agricultural laborers. Ten years later, the picture had improved somewhat: just under a third were farm workers.

The ethnic pattern of American society changed in 1965. The civil rights movement had begun to awaken the moral conscience of America, condemning racism in all its forms, including immigration laws based on race. Blacks and progressive whites joined to protest against racial discrimination, and their efforts gradually reshaped the nation's racial policies. In 1954, the U.S. Supreme Court declared that racially segregated schools were illegal. Ten years later, after countless civil rights marches and demonstrations led by the Reverend Martin Luther King, Jr., and others, Congress outlawed racial discrimination.

The next step was to ensure equal rights for immigrants who wanted to enter the United States. "Everywhere else in our national life, we have eliminated discrimination based on national origins," Robert Kennedy, attorney general of the United States, told Congress in 1964. "Yet, this system

A great number of the more recent immigrants from the Philippines are college-educated, middle-class professionals who cannot find work in the depressed economy of their homeland. Enrique Araneta is a psychiatrist who specializes in treating post-traumatic stress disorder.

is still the foundation of our immigration law." The following year, Congress passed the Immigration Act of 1965, which opened the door for a second great wave of immigrants from Asia. The 1965 law ended the old system of setting different immigration quotas for each country of origin. It allowed 20,000 people from each Asian country to enter the United States every year, up to a total of 170,000 immigrants annually. Family members of Asians who had become U.S. citizens were also free to enter the country and were not included in the annual total.

After the 1965 immigration law went into effect, Filipinos began entering the United States in large numbers. But compared with the second-wave Chinese immigrants, the recent Filipino immigrants have been "invisible." The Chinese newcomers have become concentrated in Chinatowns in large cities and have built new Chinese suburban communities, while the Filipinos have spread throughout the population. Another reason why Filipinos seem less visible in American society is that they speak Spanish and have Spanish names, and so they are sometimes confused with Hispanic Americans.

Yet the second wave of Filipino immigration has been much larger than recent Chinese immigration. Between 1965 and 1984, 665,000 Filipinos entered the United States—compared to only 465,000 Chinese. Today Filipinos are the largest Asian group in the United States, followed by the Chinese.

More than three-fourths of the Filipinos in the United States are immigrants. Unlike the early Filipino immigrants, the second-wave Filipinos have come from the city rather than the countryside, and they have migrated as settlers rather than temporary sojourners. A majority of them have become U.S. citizens. In contrast to the early immigrants, who were mostly men, the recent Filipino newcomers have been mainly women. The first-wave immigrants in the 1920s were generally poor villagers or farmers, but the new immigrants include professionals, such as engineers, scientists, accountants, teachers, lawyers, nurses, and doctors. Between 1966 and 1970, for example, only 10% of the Filipino immigrants were laborers, and 65% were professional and technical workers.

Many middle-class, well-educated Filipinos left the Philippines because of the corrupt, repressive government of President Ferdinand Marcos, who ruled the Philippines from 1965 until 1986. During this time, professionals in the Philippines grew critical of Marcos's corruption and alarmed by his violations of human rights. Amnesty International, a worldwide human rights organization, reported on the torture of political prisoners in the Philippines in 1976, prompting a Filipino stockbroker who had immigrated to the United States to remark, "I know such things to be true." A Filipino business executive told the *New York Times* that the 1983 assassination of Benigno Aquino, who led a movement against the Marcos government, was one of the major reasons why he had moved to the United States with his family. At that time, the Philippines seemed to be sinking into a reign of oppression and terrorism.

But people also emigrated from the Philippines for economic reasons. Many of those who left were highly educated but could not find skilled or professional jobs in the Philippines. Describing this "brain drain," the *Los Angeles Times* said in 1972, "There is an overabundance of a well-educated middle class in the Philippines, and a startling number of them cannot use their special learning after graduation. The Philippine government's own statistics indicate that only 60% of today's college graduates are employed in any more than menial jobs."

A very high percentage of people in the Philippines are college graduates. Many, however, have faced extremely limited prospects. In 1970, a million people had college diplomas, of which little more than half were able to find suitable employment. "We have more than two hundred registered civil engineers in the city," said the mayor of one Philippine city. "Where would I get them employed! So the problem is a surplus of professionals."

College-educated Filipinos suffered not only from a scarcity of jobs but also from low wages. "Wages in Manila are barely enough to answer for my family's needs," said one Filipino. "I must go abroad to better my chances." A nurse compared wages in the two countries: "My one day's earning here in America is more than my one month's salary in Manila, especially when I do a plus eight [overtime]." Explaining why he and other professionals had come to the United States, an accountant said, "It is common [in the Philippines] for middle-class Filipinos to work at two or even three jobs because of the high cost of living. I have paid as much as $7.50 per pound for chicken there because food is not in abundance as it is here. . . . In the United States, hard work is rewarded. In the Philippines, it is part of the struggle to survive."

Images of American abundance, carried home by the *Balikbayans,* the immigrants who return to the islands for visits, have been drawing frustrated Filipinos to the United States ever since. One man went back for a visit after working in the United States for 10 years, and he told his friends, "If you work, you'll get milk and honey in America." Other Balikbayans described the United States as a "paradise." The governor of one island province reported, "The Balikbayans say that in the United States people from the Philippines are given the opportunity to work for better pay, better medical conditions, better social security. . . . For example medical practitioners who migrate and become American citizens have very good opportunities in the United States, both personally and professionally."

Because of low wages and difficult working conditions, the profession of nursing has lost some of its attraction for those who have other options. Nurses from the Philippines have made up for the deficit and become a mainstay of the American health-care system.

Nurses and doctors have played a great part in the recent wave of immigration. Filipino nurses and doctors seem to be everywhere in the medical services in the United States. During the 1970s, one-fifth of the 20,000 nurses who graduated from school in the Philippines came to the United States. The flow of Filipino doctors has been even greater. Forty percent of all Filipino doctors in the world practice in the United States, and the medical school of the University of Santo Tomas in the Philippines has been a major supplier of doctors to the United States. By 1974, there were 7,000 Filipino doctors in the United States. There were 1,000 in New York alone, where the total Filipino population was only

45,000. Filipino doctors have been on the staff of every hospital in New York and New Jersey.

But coming to America has not necessarily increased opportunities for Filipino medical professionals. In the United States, Filipino doctors must pass an examination administered by the Educational Council for Foreign Medical Graduates in order to qualify for private practice, or hospital internship or residence. This test, as well as additional state requirements, often force Filipino doctors to do further study and find temporary work as nurses' aides and laboratory assistants. "In Los Angeles, there are several hundred Filipino unlicensed physicians working in jobs that are totally unrelated to their knowledge and expertise," Dr. Jenny Batongmalaque told the California Advisory Committee to the U.S. Commission on Civil Rights. "They have no opportunity to review or to attend review classes. They cannot afford to pay the tuition and they have no time because they have to earn a living to feed themselves and their children." A Filipino attorney told the committee, "Filipino doctors are accepted as professionals as defined by the Immigration and Naturalization Service and the Department of Labor. However, when they come here, they are not allowed to practice that profession under which they were granted the visa because of the State's strict licensing procedures. That's an inconsistency." This inconsistency forced one Filipino surgeon to work in a restaurant as a meat cutter. He did not tell his bosses that he was a doctor, but later, in an interview, he smiled as he remarked, "They thought I was very good at separating the meat from the bone."

Pharmacists educated in the Philippines have met even greater difficulties. They are not even allowed to take the licensing examinations in many states. In California, for example, only graduates of schools on the State Board of Pharmacy's approved list can take the test to receive their licenses, but that list has never included a foreign school. As a result, hundreds of Filipino pharmacists have been kept from practicing their profession.

Filipino veterinarians have also encountered obstacles. After arriving in America in 1973, a veterinarian ex-

Larry Dulary Itliong, a cannery and farm laborer who organized a protest strike by Filipino grape pickers in California in 1965. Itliong convinced Cesar Chavez, leader of the Mexican farm labor movement, to join the strike.

For the Filipinos, as for other immigrant groups, it is the children who embody their hopes for the future.

plained that she had hoped to practice in her field. But she learned that she would first have to pass an English test, satisfy a one-year clinical internship at an accredited veterinary hospital without pay, and pass the California state licensing examination. To support herself and her family while she prepared for the examination, she had to work as a clerk at an insurance company. She finally obtained her license—after seven years. "Foreign educated or trained professionals are as good as the Americans," she said in an interview, adding that she believed the licensing requirements were set up to discourage foreigners who might compete with graduates of American schools for jobs.

Many Filipino immigrants have found themselves underemployed, working at jobs far below those for which they were trained. In Salinas, California, during the 1970s, more than half of the new immigrants who had been employed in professional and technical occupations in the Philippines worked as clerks, salespeople, and wage laborers. Meeting socially, they playfully called one another by their former titles, such as "Doctor," "Professor," or "Attorney." Reported the *New York Times,* "[Filipino] lawyers work as file clerks, teachers as secretaries, dentists as aids, engineers as mechanics."

Sometimes Filipino professionals are steered toward low-level jobs simply because they are Filipino. For example, a college-educated newcomer went to a government employment office to find a job and was advised to look for work as an agricultural laborer. The disappointed job-seeker said, "He simply asked me if I were a Filipino and without opening my folder he gave me an address of a vegetable grower."

Be they old-timers or recent immigrants, Filipinos have faced a struggle to be accepted in the United States. They have confronted racial prejudice, job discrimination, and underemployment, yet their presence in America is large and growing. While they continue to seek the dream of freedom that America offers, they are helping to create a new multicultural society. Filipino immigrants have come, as Carlos Bulosan expressed it, "searching for a door into America" and seeking to build new lives. "Would it be possible," he asked, "for an immigrant like me to become part of the American dream?"

Chronology

16th century	Spain establishes the Philippine islands as a Spanish colony.
1898	The United States defeats Spain in the Spanish-American War; the Philippines become a U.S. territory.
1906	Significant numbers of Filipino immigrants begin arriving in Hawaii and the United States.
1924	A federal law bans immigration from Asia, but the law does not apply to Filipinos, who live in a U.S. territory.
1934	U.S. Congress passes the Tydings-McDuffie Act, which makes the Philippines a commonwealth and limits immigration to 50 people each year.
1935	Congress passes the Repatriation Act to encourage Filipino immigrants to return to the Philippines.
1941–45	The United States is involved in World War II; much fighting takes places in the Philippines.

1946 The Philippines become an independent nation; Filipino immigration to the U.S. is doubled to 100 people a year.

1965 The federal Immigration Act of 1965 opens the door for a second wave of immigration from Asia; Filipino immigrants begin entering the United States in large numbers.

Further Reading

Bandon, Alexandra. *Filipino Americans.* New York: Macmillan Children's Group, 1993.

Buaken, Manuel. *I Have Lived with the American People.* Caldwell, ID: Caxton, 1948.

Bulosan, Carlos. *America Is in the Heart: A Personal History.* 1946. Reprint. Seattle: University of Washington Press, 1973.

———. *If You Want To Know What We Are.* Albuquerque, NM: West End, 1983.

Cordova, Fred. *Filipinos, Forgotten Asian Americans: A Pictorial Essay.* Dubuque, IA: Kendall/Hunt, 1983.

Crouchett, Lorraine Jacobs. *Filipinos in California: From the Days of the Galleons to the Present.* El Cerrito, CA: Downey Place, 1982.

Filipino Oral History Project. *Voices: A Filipino American Oral History.* Stockton, CA: Filipino Oral History Project, 1984.

Mayberry, Jodine. *Filipinos.* New York: Franklin Watts, 1990.

Melendy, Brett. *Asians in America: Filipinos, Koreans, and East Indians.* New York: Hippocrene, 1981.

Stern, Jennifer. *The Filipino Americans.* New York: Chelsea House, 1989.

Vallangca, Caridad C. *The Second Wave: Pinay and Pinoy.* Portland, OR: Strawberry Hill, 1987.

Vallangca, Roberto V. *Pinoy: The First Wave, 1889–1941.* Portland, OR: Strawberry Hill, 1977.

Winter, Frank H. *The Filipinos in America.* Minneapolis: Lerner, 1988.

Index

PICTURE CREDITS

The Bettmann Archive: pp. 16, 19, 97; Bishop Museum Archives: p. 28; Brown Brothers: pp. 20, 23, 26; Courtesy Filipino American National Historical Society: cover, pp. 30, 34, 36, 38, 47, 76; Courtesy *FILIPINOS: Forgotten Asian Americans,* by Fred Cordova: pp. 6, 33, 41, 42, 44, 49, 52, 62, 65, 67, 70, 73, 74, 81, 83, 86, 89, 98, 104; Corky Lee: pp. 113, 116; Courtesy Ronald Takaki: p. 102; UPI/Bettmann: pp. 94, 110, 108, 115; Visual Communications: p. 57. Map by Gary Tong: p. 15.

RONALD TAKAKI, the son of immigrant plantation laborers from Japan, graduated from the College of Wooster, Ohio, and earned his Ph.D. in history from the University of California at Berkeley, where he has served both as the chairperson and the graduate advisor of the Ethnic Studies program. Professor Takaki has lectured widely on issues relating to ethnic studies and multiculturalism in the United States, Japan, and the former Soviet Union and has won several important awards for his teaching efforts. He is the author of six books, including the highly acclaimed *Strangers from a Different Shore: A History of Asian Americans,* and the recently published *A Different Mirror: A History of Multicultural America.*

REBECCA STEFOFF is a writer and editor who has published more than 50 nonfiction books for young adults. Many of her books deal with geography and exploration, including the three-volume set *Extraordinary Explorers,* recently published by Oxford University Press. Stefoff also takes an active interest in environmental issues. She served as editorial director for two Chelsea House series—*Peoples and Places of the World* and *Let's Discover Canada.* Stefoff studied English at the University of Pennsylvania, where she taught for three years. She lives in Portland, Oregon.